The Compleat Trespasser

John Bainbridge is a freelance journalist, the author of some thirty topographical books, many articles on the outdoors in magazines and newspapers. He is also well-known as a novelist. John read literature and social history at the University of East Anglia. He has been a rambler and hillwalker for over fifty years and has been commended by the Ramblers Association for his many years of voluntary work in the rambling movement. John spent nine years as chief executive of the Dartmoor Preservation Association, fending off threats to the Dartmoor National Park. He is an outspoken advocate of ramblers' rights and the freedom to roam. John is an inveterate trespasser.

The Compleat Trespasser was first published in 2014. This revised and expanded edition was first published in 2020.

The Compleat Trespasser was first published in Great Britain in 2014, This revised and expanded version was published in 2020. Copyright © J and A Bainbridge 2014/20. The right of John Bainbridge to be identified as the author of this work has been asserted by him in accordance with the Copyright, Designs and Patent Act 1988. **All rights reserved.** No part of this publication may be reproduced, stored in or introduced into a retrieval system, or transmitted, in any form, or by any means (electronic, mechanical, photocopying, recording or otherwise) without the prior written permission of the author. Any person who does any unauthorised act in relation to this publication may be liable to criminal prosecution and civil claims for damages. This publication must not be circulated in any form of binding or cover other than that in which it is now published and without a similar condition including this condition being imposed on the subsequent purchaser.

Connect with John at:

www.walkingtheoldways.wordpress.com

www.johnbainbridgewriter.wordpress.com

Books by John Bainbridge

Fiction
Balmoral Kill
Dangerous Game
The Shadow of William Quest
Deadly Quest
Dark Shadow
Loxley
Wolfshead
Villain
Legend

Non-Fiction
Wayfarer's Dole
Footloose with George Borrow
Rambling – Some Thoughts on Country Walking
Footloose in Devon

THE COMPLEAT TRESPASSER

Journeys into Forbidden Britain

No man made the land, it is the original inheritance of the whole species. The land of every country belongs to the people of that country
John Stuart Mill, 1848

John Bainbridge

Fellside Books

Contents

The right to roam 6
What the law of trespass says 8
First steps off the path 10
Where you can walk now 14
The importance of paths 16
Straying further 19
When the restrictions began 24
Through well-keepered ground 26
Enclosures and game-preserves 30
Woodlands – Keep Out! 32
A woodland trespass 38
Forbidden lands 43
Trespassing in Scotland 47
Access battles in the Lake District 54
Ten thousand trespassers on Winter Hill 66
Two poets and a gamekeeper 68
Delight on a shiny night 71
We'll fight in the hills 75
The Trespasser's Walk 79
Sacred land 84
The paths to Kinder Scout 86
Trespassing on the great estates 90
The Kinder Scout Mass Trespass 96
The Battle of Abbey Brook 100
Notes for prospective trespassers 102
Forbidden Britain 106
Useful organisations 108
Recommended reading 109

The Compleat Trespasser

Wandering the countryside by day and night, rambling through dark forests and quiet meadows. Climbing mountains and roving the lonely moorlands. Sleeping nights in the hollows between rocks or in the shelter of a tree. Exploring the lands beyond the Keep Out *notices, going into the forbidden wooded coverts of the great estates, rambling down the rides and paths that are out of bounds - where a gamekeeper might take a shot at you. Making friends with vagabonds. Fighting to preserve the ancient lines of pathways. Journeying in the steps of those who have gone before. Recognising that the land is the common heritage of all people and that we should all own the right to roam. That is the Trespasser's creed...*

The Right to Roam

Whether or not to trespass in the British countryside?

That always has to be an individual choice. But it has to be noted that many of the rights of countryside access that we all enjoy today - not least our right to walk in the British countryside at all - are only there because people stretched the letter of the law by trespassing.

We would probably never have had the *Countryside and Rights of Way Act* in 2000, the *Scottish Land Reform Act* in 2003, our National Parks, or even many of our footpaths and bridleways, but for those pioneer ramblers who pushed the boundaries. Particularly those who mass trespassed at Kinder Scout and Abbey Brook in the Peak District in 1932, or the ramblers who have walked individually on the forbidden lands of these islands over decades of recent British history.

There is a long and historic tradition of trespassing in Britain. It is a hugely important part of this country's social history.

Trespassing as an art has been practised by a great many famous names; the poet William Wordsworth trespassed, as did the first Labour Prime Minister Ramsay MacDonald. So did Tory Prime Minister Winston Churchill. The composer Sir Michael Tippett, the songwriter Ewan McColl, the historian A.J.P. Taylor, the philosopher C.E.M. Joad, the famous guide book writer Alfred Wainwright – all wandered away from the not so straight and narrow to reclaim the countryside. There have been many others, household names and unknowns.

Every day in our countryside, local people and visitors wander into fields and woodlands where they have no legal right to be. They wander in this free manner by tradition, habit, custom – call it what you like. If you spend any time at all in our countryside, it is hard not to do it.

I confess to being an inveterate trespasser. That is my choice. Do you feel the urge to follow in my footsteps? **Then on your own head be it!** *You take all responsibility for your actions entirely upon yourself and must be prepared to accept any consequences.* Think carefully before you stray away from the country lane, the bridleway or the public footpath. Consider the penalties…

But then why shouldn't the British people have free access to the best bits of our own countryside? Many of our parents and grandparents fought for this country in the World Wars. Some of my readers may well have served in more recent conflicts.

Why is it deemed okay to be prepared to die for your country, but not be allowed to walk across it? Why should returning war veterans be deemed trespassers for wanting to enjoy the best of our countryside? The people of Scotland now have a very enlightened land reform legislation, which gives people the legal right to wander almost anywhere, with a few common sense exceptions. But how long will it be before the English, Welsh and Irish have the same basic human right?

If the very idea of trespassing appals you, then please stop reading now. Though perhaps you might continue and give me a fair hearing. If trespassing is not for you, then I quite understand. Do stay on the public rights of way and the country lanes. There is a great deal of joy to be had in wandering along those pleasant byways. You might find my other walking books a help and more to your taste, should you want to pursue a course of more legitimate country walking.

Or you may decide to be an armchair trespasser, taking in some of the adventures that follow in this book and the writings of others. Perhaps feeling a quiet sympathy but staying firmly indoors. And that is fine. There is a great deal of pleasure to be had from reading about our lovely countryside. I adore reading such accounts myself. Vicarious roaming can be quite thrilling. Many of our finest country writers have published their own adventures.

But should you decide to go further and wander off the not so straight and narrow byways of the British countryside, then good luck to you! You are in a noble tradition…

What the Law of Trespass says

The people of England and Wales do not have the general access enjoyed by walkers in Scotland. Walk away from public rights of way or access land and you are trespassing.

But the "Trespassers Will Be Prosecuted" signs you see here and there are pretty meaningless in law. With some exceptions, trespassing in England and Wales is a tort, a civil matter and not a criminal offence. Which means you can't be prosecuted unless you cause damage. Trespass is a criminal offence if you trespass in places like the royal estates, military training grounds and establishments, railways etc.

Should you cause damage, the landowner might sue you in the civil courts. But it would have to be a proven and measurable damage. Simply walking through a woodland track or bending down a bit of grass probably wouldn't count and certainly wouldn't be worth suing for, though you could be liable for the landowner's legal costs if they wanted to take the gamble.

However, if you force your way through a hedgerow, break a gate or damage a fence etc., the landowner might be able to claim damages. If your actions cause livestock to roam and an animal is lost or injured, then the damages could be considerable. Please bear this in mind before deciding to wander away from rights of way.

Landowners also have a right in law to physically remove you from their land, though only if they use reasonable force, and if you have refused to depart. If they challenge you, they can insist that you leave their land forthwith. But they can only make you go to the nearest public highway; i.e. road, footpath, bridleway etc. These are just very brief guidance notes on trespassing and should not be taken as legal definitions.

Please consult the Blue Book (see below) if you want an absolutely definitive ruling on trespassing matters. As I understand the law, you are not obliged to give a landowner your name and address. If you trespass persistently on one stretch of land, then there is a chance that the landowner might take out a court injunction against you. If you trespass there after that, you would be in contempt of court and could be gaoled.

The above comments are a very brief introduction to path law and land access in England and Wales and the comments made above are a guide only. *They should not be taken as definitive.* If you want a more detailed explanation then please do visit the Ramblers website www.ramblers.org.uk

The classic book on rights of way law is what is called 'the Blue Book': its title being *Rights of Way: a guide to law and practice* published jointly by the Ramblers and the Open Spaces Society. If you are interested in footpath work and your right to walk, it is the one to get. It is usually accepted as the definitive answer to any legal matter relating to access.

First steps off the path

I have always wandered where I like in our countryside.

If the mood takes me then off I go, though always with care and consideration. It has always been that way. Boys in my time were trespassers by nature. It simply didn't occur to me, when I was young, that people could own vast tracts of countryside to the exclusion of all others. I roamed the fields, climbed the hills and sat by the river banks without a notion of what the word trespass meant.

I didn't know it then, but I shared these trespassing tastes with some famous and reputable forebears. In his remarkable essay *In Praise of Walking*, Sir Leslie Stephen, writer, philosopher, first editor of the *Dictionary of National Biography*, and the father of the novelist Virginia Woolf, made no bones about his enthusiasm for trespass when out on his long country walks

When once beyond the "town," I looked for notices that trespassers would be prosecuted, that gave a strong presumption that the trespass must have some attraction. To me it was a reminder of the many delicious bits of walking which, even in the neighbourhood of London, await the man who has no superstitious reverence for legal rights. It is indeed surprising how many charming walks can be contrived by a judicious combination of a little trespassing with the rights of way happily preserved over so many commons and footpaths.

Stephen was the founding member of a rather intellectual Victorian rambling club called the 'Sunday Tramps' which organised long walks, initially from Stephen's house at Wimbledon and then, as the ramblers grew more ambitious, from country railway stations to some worthwhile destination, or back into London. Well-known figures from Victorian literary society and the scientific and legal establishment were to join the Sunday Tramps, including the novelist George Meredith and the lawyer Sir Frederick Pollock.

The object of the group was not just walking but engagement in cerebral talk, leading George Meredith to recollect that 'there was conversation which would have made the presence of a shorthand writer a benefactor to the country.' The Tramps would halt for sustenance at the home of one member or another, though Sir Leslie Stephen considered this to be "pampering" and would usually insist on them seeking out bread and ale at some lowly wayside inn.

Despite coming from the propertied classes, the attitude of the Sunday Tramps towards trespass is fascinating. Supporting Stephen's contention that *there should be no superstitious reverence for legal rights*, the Sunday Tramps trespassed on a regular basis as part of their walks. Such was the frequency of these misdemeanours, that a formula was devised which they might present to any challenging landowner or gamekeeper. Many years later one member recalled that

They avoided high roads and trespassed, if necessary, discreetly over private property in their pursuit of short cuts or the fairest bits of the countryside. And it is due to the ingenuity of Sir Frederick Pollock, acting we believe, on a hint from no less an authority than Lord Bramwell, that the following legal formula was invented for the Tramps when called upon to deal with any troublesome gamekeeper or owner presuming to warn them off his property: 'We hereby give you notice that we do not, nor doth any of us, claim any right of way or other easement into or over these lands, and we tender you this shilling by way of amends'. It should be noted that this formula is most effective when repeated, after the leader, in solemn chant by a large party of Tramps.

I've always shared the Sunday Tramps' contempt for trespass notices, though I've never thought to offer a shilling to a gamekeeper. I've never tramped in such exalted company as the Sunday Tramps, though I've had some fine companions on my more legitimate rambles. A trespass, I feel, is better conducted alone. It is easier to deal with any problems that might occur if you have only yourself to look out for.

My vagabonding adventures have recognised few exclusion zones. As a boy I brushed aside the *No Trespassing* notices as though they were not there, not really understanding what the words meant. Now I understand so very well but apply my own discretion as to whether or not I have a right to roam.

I can't remember whether my boyhood routes were public rights of way or not, for there were no such things then as signposts or waymarked paths in my neck of the woods. I didn't know what a footpath or bridleway was. I'd no map. I learned the landscape by repeated experience.

Sometimes I would see a farmer or his labourers harvesting a field close to home, but they seemed friendly folk and never objected to me being there. I never walked through their growing crops, but only on fallow ground, field boundaries and existing tracks. The farmer and his workers would wave, stop for a yarn and let me help on harvest days. I lived for the weekends when I might walk and explore from dawn to dusk, edging ever further out, like a wild animal seeking to find a break in an obstructing perimeter fence.

I was twelve before I realised that some landowners didn't want people on their land. I walked the four miles to school, along tracks and paths that wound under the canal and into untended fields, meant even then for development and urban sprawl. It was a land unloved and I felt uneasy as I climbed the long slope that led to the school lane.

There was a rackety old farmhouse, its roof tumbled and many of the windows boarded up. I'd passed it many times before and always shuddered at the sight of so much dereliction. It seemed uninhabited, despite the occasional pathetic wisp of smoke coming from its chimney.

This time, I noticed a man leaning against a wall bounding the farmyard. A little man, with a battered felt hat and grubby jacket, his trousers held up by string. I'd almost reached the gate into the lane before he leapt out, furiously waving his stick and yelling something unintelligible.

He ran after me, spitting out words that would become familiar: "Get off my land". His hat flew off to reveal grey straggly hair and a forehead covered in warts. I paused for a moment and faced him. He stopped and held the stick over his head. "This is private! This is my land! Get off!" He advanced again, waving the stick in front of him, a fierce expression on that scarred old face.

"Get out! Get out!" Like some fierce old bird uttering a warning cry.

"But I always come this way," I replied.

"Get out! Get out!"

He darted forward and crashed the stick down on my shoulder, almost screaming the words "now get out!" as he forced me backwards on to the lane. He turned away and walked back towards the ruin without a further word, as though the business between us was concluded. I staggered towards the school, my uniform askew. This was my first encounter with a hostile landowner.

It was not to be my last.

I've remained an inveterate trespasser, believing that the land is the common heritage of us all. Our countryside should be accessible without unreasonable restrictions. I've walked where I like, but always with reverence and care. I need the countryside. Walking for me is not just the outward experience of exploration, but an inward journey into the mind that perceives the joyful scene all around and its links with our history and literature.

I wandered freely across my childhood land, as indeed most of my contemporaries did, for the concepts of trespass and public rights of way were unknown to us. I suspect that it was this early conditioning that turned me into the inveterate trespasser of later years for, to quote Sir Leslie Stephen, I have no 'superstitious reverence' for absolute rights to property.

I grew up in a freer world; the country landowners of my childhood landscape would have had to turn many a blind eye to roaming locals. A great many ferocious people lived in this countryside on the edge of the Black Country. It would have been a mistake to get on the wrong side of any one of them.

Where you can walk now

There is already limited access to the countryside of England and Wales. In Scotland, people enjoy almost complete freedom to roam. Ireland is a bag of mixed fortunes for the wanderer. Here is a brief summary:

England and Wales have a network of public footpaths and bridleways to enable you to access some parts of our countryside. Most of these paths have evolved over centuries and can lead you to some fascinating places. Footpaths and bridleways are public highways under law – the *Queen's Highway* - to use the legal term, just the same as other roads. ***You are legally entitled to walk upon them***. The law also says that they should be properly signposted, not obstructed and kept clear of growth. With a few exceptions only permitted traffic is allowed on them, such as:

Footpaths: These are available to walkers *only*.

Bridleways: May be accessed by walkers, horse-riders and bicycles.

Permissive Paths: Some landowners have opened up permissive paths. These are not rights of way and you have no legal right to use them. You are there only under the tolerance of the landowner. They may be closed at any time.

BOATS (bridleways open to all traffic): These are essentially bridleways that may be accessed by motor vehicles though, unlike country lanes, they are essentially for walkers, riders and horse-drawn vehicles.

Freedom to Roam: In addition to the public paths network, you have a legal right to roam (in England and Wales) under the *Countryside and Rights of Way Act 2000* – commonly known as CRoW - on uncultivated mountain and moorland, common land, heath and downland. In addition, some Forestry Commission forests and National Nature Reserves have been added. Some landowners have dedicated land as access land under the Act. Such areas may be closed by landowners for up to 28 days per year so please check locally. Access land is marked by a yellow wash on Ordnance Survey maps.

The Ramblers Association has won its campaign for complete access to the English Coast (it already exists in Wales). An all-England coastal path is under construction.

CRoW sounds good. It is certainly an improvement on the situation that existed prior to 2000. But the amount of our countryside opened up is really a very small percentage of the total.

Access in Scotland: The Scottish land access situation is very different from that in England and Wales. The *Land Reform Act (Scotland) 2003* gives walkers a near absolute legal right to roam except in certain cases, such as away from the gardens and immediate policies of houses, and some government land. Paths tend not to be shown in the same way on Ordnance Survey maps. But there are rights of way in Scotland and a number of walking trails. If you walk at all in Scotland then please support ScotWays (the Scottish Rights of Way and Access Society) and Ramblers Scotland. Both have very useful websites which give a great deal of information on access, paths to walk and suggested routes.

Ireland: While there seems to be *de facto* access to the more popular walking areas of Ireland, tales abound of restrictions and downright hostility from some farmers and landowners.

For further information please visit the website of Mountaineering Ireland at http://www.mountaineering.ie If you are Irish or visit Ireland, please support their campaigns for improved access. The Irish and Northern Ireland tourist boards have lots of information on walking routes and accommodation. There are a number of walking guides to Eire and Northern Ireland so I presume that the walking routes therein are okay to walk. A great many people in Ireland trespass – in many areas they have little choice if they fancy a walk in the countryside.

The Importance of Paths

We all use paths to access the countryside, whether we consider ourselves ramblers or just use them as somewhere to walk the dog. Or sometimes as a short-cut, the easiest way to get from one place to another. We may well notice our surroundings, the places we walk through, but how many of us consider just why the path is there, why it even exists?

People in this country are fortunate to have a splendid network of public footpaths and bridleways to enjoy. To many walkers and riders they're something we take for granted. They've always been there and we assume they always will be. Just a convenience really.

But every step we take along a path is a stride into our own history. The ridge paths of England were in use even before the Iron Age, already centuries old when Alfred the Great marched his armies along them. That footpath you walk across a field might be the remnants of a Roman road or a medieval drovers' track. Wayside shrines by old tracks show us the way pilgrims travelled. Paths on our coastline were used by coastguards and smugglers. A path to a country church may well have been walked by worshippers for a thousand years…

Our own history is everywhere on a country ramble.

Our paths are as vitally important for telling us about the social history of Britain as archaeological sites such as Avebury and Stonehenge. Walk a path and you are walking in the steps of countless generations, who walked the same way either for work or, like us, for pleasure. These paths are the happy accidents of history.

But unlike stone circles and prehistoric burial grounds, their historical reasons for being tend to be neglected. For they are the ways of the common folk, the routes many of our own ancestors used for all sorts of purposes.

I've been a campaigner for paths for over fifty years. I've been a volunteer in the Ramblers for almost as long, serving in many posts including being an area footpath secretary and a group footpath officer. Paths are my passion. I've written about them in my own walking books and even mentioned them in my novels. But like many walkers, I took them for granted in the early days. They were just the ways into the places I wanted to walk.

At public footpath inquiries, where I represented the Ramblers, the opposition would often say, as they tried to shut or badly divert a path "Oh, it's only the way people used to walk to church, or to the next village" and so on.

But, as a social historian, that to me is very important. We *should* know about the way our forebears moved around their own land. Knowing that is every bit as crucial to our understanding of the past as interpreting the reasons why Stonehenge was built.

Losing a path, either through a closure or a poor diversion, or not recognising that it *is* a right of way, is interfering with our island story. That is why I believe the original routes of our path should be preserved as much as possible. It's our heritage and, like any other archaeology, we have a duty to save our paths for future generations.

Fortunately, many of our footpaths and bridleways are recorded on definitive and Ordnance Survey maps. But we know that many were omitted, some deliberately and others because people – although they'd always used them –never thought that they were rights of way at all. Claiming these lost paths, before the deadline of 2026, is a fight against time. It is vital that we seek out these lost paths and claim them while we can.

Back in the 1930s, the writer and author A.J. Brown – a great campaigner for access – tried to define what were historical routes. He came up with a short list

- *Ancient British ridgeways (followed by hillside ways).*
- *Romanised roads (i.e. ancient British ways. metalled and straightened by the Romans).*
- *Pure Roman roads.*
- *Drovers' roads, drift ways and pannier-mule tracks.*
- *Local green ways.*
- *Monks' Trods leading from monastery to monastery or chantry.*
- *Saltways, flintways and other local 'tradeways'.*

I would add the following to Brown's list:

- *Coffin Paths or Corpse Roads (Lich or Lyke Ways) – the way the dead were taken for burial.*
- *Parish Paths – used to get to local churches, or from farm to farm and village to village.*
- *Industrial Paths, the ways miners and quarrymen got to their work or transported minerals.*

- *Paths between industrial sites and the way workers walked to work.*
- *Paths constructed for the defence of our country in time of war.*

To this long list, we can now add paths that came about just for the sheer pleasure of walking. In my time, I've seen paths created where none had previously existed, to cater for the needs of ramblers and horse riders, often to fill in gaps on long-distance trails or to get walkers away from busy roads.

Paths are not just a luxury in our busy age, but a necessity now for our leisure. Over the past two hundred years, rambling has become a path-creating and preserving industry in its own right.

Thanks to the Ramblers and other footpath groups, we still have so many historical paths crossing the land. But there is a lot of work to do to recognise the importance of paths and to discover those ways that go unrecorded. Our politicians and planners still don't really recognise our rights of way network as a vital national resource.

There's still a lot of hard work but it is so worthwhile. For I'm always mindful of the wise words of the Victorian country chronicler Richard Jefferies, who said

Always get over a stile is the one rule that should be borne in mind by those who wish to see the land as it really is – that is to say, never omit to explore a footpath, for never was there a footpath yet which did not pass something of interest.

Straying Further

It's not as though you always set out to trespass.

The majority of my trespassing adventures have been unplanned, occurring during an ordinary and more legitimate walk in our countryside. At some point you wander away from the road or the public right of way. These unplanned diversions can lead to unexpected delights.

Walking along an ancient ridge path, I went astray in just such a fashion and found myself trespassing. The adventure was an eye-opener - a gorgeous tramp across beautiful countryside. I'd set out from a village hidden deep in a green and wooded valley, to the ringing of the bells from a church that dates back to Saxon times.

A steep climb up a public footpath brought me to the edge of a long hill, an ascent as heavy as you might find anywhere, which left me breathless by its woody summit. It was a peaceful spring morning with clear views across a broad agricultural vale to an Iron Age hill fort, a good mile away.

Coming up through the wood, I'd found a number of earth banks hidden amongst the trees, abandoned land boundaries that probably date to medieval times, perhaps even to the centuries when Saxon farmers worked this land. The hill fort itself, an expression of a desire to control, stamping the authority of man's ownership on the face of the earth, warning passers-by that their presence was only tolerated.

The path along the ridge was testament to the fact that people had journeyed this way from the earliest of times, and is probably contemporary with the hill fort, maybe even older. Folk have journeyed atop the hill for thousands of years. Tinkers and merchants have plied their trade at the farms and hamlets along its way. Gypsies have used its hidden route to seek out camp sites where they might not be disturbed, soldiers have marched, and pilgrims talked of spiritual and temporal matters as they made their journey to other and longer pilgrim routes.

Once past the wood and a stretch of open heathland, the ridge way progresses along the highest portion of the hill, passing between the high hedgerows of farm fields.

A double gate lay across the old bridleway, leading into a farmyard, crammed with cows brought in for milking. A collie dog yapped and ran up to greet me, his body low to the ground as though uncertain as to the reception he might get.

"He's all right," said the farmer as he came out of the shippon. "A good day for a walk!" He was a small, grizzled man, dressed in old country clothes of tweed and cord, a battered hat over greying hair.

"Going far?"

I explained my route and he nodded. "That's a good stretch. Don't get so many on this path now. I reckon they don't like the hill. Pity, 'cos I enjoy a bit of company. Good to see walkers about, taking an interest in the countryside. Used to do a lot myself, for pleasure as well as about the farm."

I asked about the ridge way itself. "Well, they say it's one of the oldest paths in the county and I can believe it. We've found many an old coin when we've been ploughing. My grandfer could remember drovers coming this way, taking the beasts hundreds of miles to market. They used to spend the night in our barn and keep the cattle in the yard here. All different now and not for the better. Don't like the thought of animals in lorries."

He waved me on my way with a cheerful "have a good walk." Soon after his farm, the ridge way became a metalled lane, but clearly following its traditional route.

Between the gateways were wide views over the surrounding countryside. He was obviously a farmer who cared for his rights of way, for the footpaths I followed as I left the old track, and headed down into the valley, were in an immaculate condition, clearly waymarked with good stiles and free of overgrowth. I wandered for a while alongside a tiny stream that gives a seaside town its name, before heading uphill to the opposite ridge.

A few hundred yards led to an ancient crossing, where my path was bisected by a present-day bridlepath, overgrown with gorse and bracken, but passable. It widened as I walked, clinging to the edge of the down, above a deep and wooded valley. Sheep grazed the open ground to my right, strolling away as I came near to them, moving away faster as I disturbed pheasants clustering in the surrounding undergrowth. Bird song filled the air, though I saw few, thanks to the thickness of the leaves on the nearby trees.

There were pheasants now in profusion, suggesting that I'd entered the preserves of a shooting estate, though the bridleway was clearly waymarked and obviously well used. Woodlands of oak and beech lined the valley eastwards and alongside the track were several deep goyles, natural cuttings into the chalky ground, widened by the men of the past who must have sought stone and flints from their precipitous slopes.

It was a wonderful section of ancient ridgeway and it wasn't hard to imagine the travellers of old as they journeyed on foot or horseback. There was little gradient to my route, a barely perceptible descent that would be scarcely noticed. There were occasional glimpses of the sea, suggesting that the path may have had its origins, in prehistoric times, in expeditions to find salt for the preservation of meat.

As I wandered downhill, the track followed round a slight curve of the hill, a path going off to the right. This section was more wooded and I noticed a number of pheasant pens amid its little glades. I paused to look back the way I'd come, such was the beauty of the path and the glory of the trees along the way.

It didn't occur to me at first that I was no longer following the bridleway. Only a change in the position of the sun and the distant coastline suggested that I was heading in the wrong direction. I dug into my knapsack and pulled out the map. There it was, the line of the ridge way, very clearly marked. I found the farm and the lane beyond. Then the truth dawned. The bridleway did *not* follow the ridge way beyond the curve where the tiny path had led off to the right.

At some point in history, the right of way had been removed from this most ancient route of passage. I looked at the alternative path on the map. It seemed purely functional, running along the edge of a field and out on to a road. Functional and artificial, a convenience more for the landowner than the tramper.

Yet here I was in the midst of beautiful countryside and obviously on what had been the ridgeway of old. Why had this right of way been stolen from the people? I determined to find out. The woods were thicker now and the pheasants numerous. A number of pleasing rides led down through the woods, but there were other paths as well. Narrower routes across the valley to the east. And on one of these, I found the stump of what might once have been a fingerpost, one of those delightful signs that mark the course of a public footpath.

So in past times there had been other rights of way around this estate. People had once enjoyed the freedom to roam over paths beyond the ridgeway. And not that long ago, judging by the evidence of the old footpath sign. Perhaps even since the local map of all rights of way had been compiled in the 1950s.

I took out the Ordnance Survey sheet and searched in vain for the slightest evidence that any rights of way existed now. But the truth dawned clear. At some time a ridge way and all of its ancillary paths, tracks that people had walked for thousands of years, had been barred to the public.

I soon found out why.

The next curve of the track opened up a wider vista across the valley. There was a Georgian manor house, surrounded by a formal garden. As I looked across to the wooded coverts on the opposite side of the valley, it became obvious that one landowner had created a little world of exclusion for his own benefit. It was certainly an idyllic spot, though I suspected that sporting rights were the real reason that access to the ridgeway was denied. The pens and feeders suggested that the pheasant breeding was on a commercial scale. This was not one man's retreat. It was a rural business on an industrial scale.

Yet the pheasants scampered around my feet, almost oblivious to my presence. They are not much bothered by walkers, or easily disturbed at all. It's hard enough for the beaters on a shoot to get pheasants to take to the air. The bird's preference is always to scuttle into the nearest bit of undergrowth. A great party of walkers would have no effect on any shoot, particularly as they would be on defined paths as they made their way through the coverts. No landowner or keeper can seriously deny this.

And it's no good them suggesting that public access might lead to theft or poaching. I have known a few thieves and many a poacher in my time. None were bothered about whether or not they were following rights of way. No one challenged me as I walked down the ridge way. I could easily have made off with a dozen pheasants.

The ridge way ended on the concreted drive to the house and I followed this up to a public highway. I was some distance from where I wanted to be, but a glance at the map showed that I could get there by a couple of miles of lane walking. It was pleasant too, offering good views across the countryside and down into the private grounds of the manor.

After a mile, I came across another hill fort from the Iron Age. Wooded now, its banks and ditches still covered by the last autumn's leaves. There was public access here and several people could be seen picnicking or just wandering around. But to me, these vast earthworks survive in curious isolation, for today's visitors can no longer walk freely along its prehistoric access routes.

Or those paths which were old before the hill fort existed.

When the Restrictions Began

Robin Hood was one of my boyhood heroes.

He still is, now I am much longer in years. I'm sure that reading his adventures, watching the many films and television series and dreaming of life in the greenwood, inspired me to have such contempt for these absolute rules of property.

The ones that dictate that the British are barred from much of their own countryside and heritage.

There is something rather wonderful about a defender of the poor and dispossessed. Someone taking the side of those who have next to nothing. Fighting the powerful and corrupt.

We should all do it.

In a way, the world is still divided into the supporters of Robin Hood and those who back the Sheriff of Nottingham. Currently, the Sheriff's backers have the upper hand, both politically and in the financial system that rules our lives. Greed and selfishness are the motives that seem to inspire the people who run modern Britain. They would even try to deny you the land, which as John Stuart Mill says, is the "common heritage of us all."

Trespassing is a way of cocking a snook at this awful philosophy.

I mentioned Robin Hood because I want to examine how the Normans inflicted land access restrictions on us all. In the Robin Hood ballads, and the various modern interpretations of the old tales, you will recall that the Norman overlords restrict access to the land – in this case Sherwood Forest.

This triggers all of the outlawry and conflict.

It is a true picture of life under the Normans.

Prior to the Norman Conquest in 1066, it seems that people could more or less wander where they liked, without let or hindrance. The Anglo-Saxons, who ruled before, had a much more live and let live philosophy.

But how it all changed on that October day, a few miles out of Hastings.

Within one generation, vast restrictions were placed on what you could do in our countryside and where you could go. Sadly, these restrictions, rather than the more amenable Saxon freedoms, have lasted a thousand years. They are the root cause of much that is wrong with our society. And everything that is immoral about the British attitude to land ownership and access. In more than one way, those Norman overlords are still with us.

It was the Norman love of hunting that caused the rot to set in. About a quarter of England was dedicated as hunting Forests (held by the Crown) and hunting Chases (held by other powerful Normans). This land was set aside, in the years following the Conquest, for the benefit of the few, not the many. Whole towns and villages vanished from the map to make way for this love of venery.

Hundreds of thousands of people were cleared away, as though they were of no consequence at all. Uncountable thousands were massacred or driven to starvation. Those who resisted were outlawed – literally put beyond the protection of the law – a price put on their heads, just as if they were wolves. There to be killed, blinded or mutilated at the whim of the new landowners. At the mercy of everyone who wanted to earn a reward, overlord or collaborator. It was against the background of this holocaust that the outlaw ballads of Robin Hood began.

The whole nature of the way Britons related to the land was changed for ever. Forbidden Britain was born. The presumption became that the majority were forbidden access to land, now controlled by a very small minority. As the centuries passed, trespassers were considered to be the successors of those original outlaws. Fair game for landowners, gamekeepers, and the powers that be. As we shall see later, the situation didn't improve with the passage of time…

Through Well-Keepered Ground

We saw the gamekeeper long before he saw us.

We watched as he climbed the steep meadow below the oakwood, looking languidly from side to side towards the trees that swept down to the boundaries of the open ground. He wore an ancient tweed jacket, a shotgun broken over the crook of his arm. Far below were the sprawling buildings of the country house and estate, enclaved within the wild boundaries of the Great Estate.

High summer and the leaves and bracken hid us from his view, as we trespassed in his preserves. It was the middle of the afternoon and the air was still. We threw ourselves down across the roots of an oak, the better to watch a fox carrying out a desultory, diurnal hunt along the edge of these strictly private pheasant preserves. It was, perhaps, the fox that the keeper was seeking out, though it had melted into the undergrowth as it picked up the scent of the keeper on the hillside. The keeper was to shoot a different prey on that long summer day.

Jack and I were trespassers by nature, recognising no boundaries in our quest to explore the countryside. By those teenage years, little of the Devon countryside was unknown to us, from the high moorlands of Dartmoor to the marshes of the River Exe. Old tracks, some dating to the Iron Age, had been followed. We knew the line of most of the footpaths and bridleways that led from farm hamlet to village church, the winding routes of a hundred green lanes, and the secret animal paths in the local copses.

We were known to a great many countrymen, many of whom took time to show us the secrets of the countryside, the rare birds and animals that usually take years of experience to see. We had all the time in the world for these rural explorations. Jack's job was undemanding, an apprenticeship that gave him lots of time off. I was on the dole.

Each morning we would set out on a long day's adventuring, sometimes covering thirty miles before evening. We were poor, but we were free. We dressed as wretchedly as the tramps that haunted the quieter byways of the county in those days, a simple lunch carried in old army knapsacks which would be slung on our backs, or as often across our shoulders. Our boots were the cheapest refugees of the army-surplus store, and we had a taste for battered old hats and mighty walking sticks.

We were aware of the Great Estate, a huge enclosed area of woodland and open parkland. There were no rights of way and public access was severely discouraged. We'd heard tales of local poachers being dragged before the magistrates or being given a beating. But its woodlands were inviting, deep and green in the height of summer and every permutation of red and brown in the Devon autumn.

A narrow and not often used lane ran alongside the estate boundary, complete with regular warning signs informing that "Trespassers Will Be Prosecuted". There was no wall, just a verge from the road and a tiny earth bank, topped with wire. Apart from all of this deterring paraphernalia, the forbidden lands of the Great Estate looked little different from the open woodland on the other side of the lane.

For two trampers who had the very human desire to know every inch of their local countryside, the temptations of the Great Estate were too hard to resist. On one long hard tramp over Dartmoor, we debated the dangers and difficulties of invading this forbidden land. It was not that we hadn't trespassed very frequently. We had. But not over such well-keepered ground. It took three attempts before we found ourselves inside the boundary fence. Three walks almost around the entire perimeter of the prohibited territory.

Then, one evening, after sitting quietly to make sure that there were no keepers concealed, we crossed the verge, the ditch, the bank and the boundary fence. A narrow deer path led invitingly into the heart of the woodland, which we followed for a few hundred yards into the oakwoods, before our nerve failed as we put up a brace of pheasants that tore, protesting, into the air. We gasped for breath as we regained the safety of the lane. But even a glimpse of that delightful forest had been enough - we were determined to return.

The following Saturday afternoon we made our way back along the lane to the spot where we had beaten such a hasty retreat. It was a balmy, windless day, and the leaves of the tree canopy kept away the greater heat of the sun.

There was no one around as we crossed the fence and followed the now-familiar path into the woods. In the middle of the day, we put up no pheasants. They had obviously sought shelter from the sun in the deeper undergrowth. But as we progressed along the path to the edge of the trees, we caught a glimpse of deer grazing on the opposite hillside. We saw their heads turn as they spotted the fox and watched them retreat into distant woodland as the keeper came into view.

I'm still not quite sure how the keeper became aware we were there. He seemed to be walking a determined course up the valley and was way below us, when he turned suddenly and headed very swiftly in our direction, striding uphill and ramming his shotgun closed as he moved. It is possible that we disturbed some birds and he mistook us for the fox.

Had we headed into the trees and laid low, he might have passed us by on the path. But as he came within a few hundred yards, he had a full view of the both of us. He stood still for a brief moment and yelled a challenge, bringing the gun up to his shoulder.

I never heard the bang of the gun, but just felt the stings of what seemed a thousand heavy hornets as the pellets hit my right arm and leg. I recollect falling backwards into a pile of old leaves. I'd been half-hidden by an oak, which had absorbed much of the shot. But I can remember, even now, how clear my mind was at that moment and the urgent feeling that we must escape in case he fired again. Jack was unhurt and I felt nothing as we stumbled up the path. As I half-fell over the boundary fence and into the ditch, Jack pulled me up. We dived across the lane and into the sanctuary of the public woodland on the other side.

Jack scouted back to the lane, before coming back to report that there was no sign of the keeper. When I think back on the incident, I feel sure he had had no deliberate intention to actually shoot me. It was a warning shot that had gone wrong, sent askew by the keeper's position lower down the gradient. I'd been at the edge of the range of his gun and little permanent harm could have been done at that distance.

I'd been peppered with shot, though my heavy walking clothes had absorbed much of the load, as had the army knapsack which hung low over my body. My right arm had caught the worst of it. There were several puncture wounds, though not much blood until we tried digging the lead out with my penknife - a mostly successful operation.

I resisted Jack's suggestion that we head for a hospital or the constabulary. Both options seemed most unsporting. Trespassing was a game we played, and we had to abide both by its rules and consequences.

We walked the dozen miles home. I was heavy-footed, and dazed after the immediate clarity of the incident, relying for a great deal of support on my walking staff. I slept heavily that night and felt little the worse for wear the next day.

In the months that followed, we avoided the countryside around the Great Estate. But that winter, I felt the challenge of another trespass lure me back. The trees were bare and there was little cover. In a long day's walking, I saw no one and there was no feeling of threat. In the several years that followed, I went back many times but without a sight of the gamekeeper.

I have not been back to those still prohibited woodlands now for these many years, having found new territory to explore in my country walks.

But that shotgun blast did more than anything else to confirm me as an incorrigible trespasser. I love the more legitimate country walks, but still get a thrill from my illicit intrusions on to land where the public is denied access - some of the grandest parts of the British Isles. But I always walk with care and awareness that there might be hostile landowners and keepers.

And as I walk, I sometimes glance at the scar on my arm, the only physical reminder of my encounter with the gamekeeper of a Devon oakwood.

Enclosures, Game Preserves and Further Restrictions

All persons found wandering abroad, lying, lodging, or being in any barn, outhouse, or in the open air, and not giving a good account of themselves, will be apprehended as rogues and vagabonds, and be either publicly whipt or sent to the house of correction, and afterwards disposed of according to law, by order of the magistrates. Any person who shall apprehend any rogue or vagabond will be entitled to a reward of ten shillings. A notice seen in late Victorian times by the country writer Richard Jefferies.

Despite the worst excesses of the Normans and their successors, there was access to most land until fairly recently in our history. Much of the countryside, to which we are now denied access, was open to all, just a couple of centuries ago.

The rot set in with the Enclosures; the land grabbing of open heaths and commons, the creation of new field boundaries over pastoral countryside, when what had once been the common weald of the majority became the private and forbidden property of the few.

To hundreds of thousands of rural dwellers, many unlettered, this must have been a baffling intrusion into the way they lived their lives. You get a flavour of it in the peasant poetry of John Clare. Decisions made in Parliament affected the majority of Britons, who were not allowed any say in the matter. It wrecked the quality of many lives – which were not usually great in the first place – and caused starvation and displacement from the land.

It was grand larceny by the few from the many, on an epic scale.

As if this were not bad enough, the heirs of the Norman overlords, and the Industrial Revolution's *nouveau riche*, many of whom couldn't wait to jump on the patrician bandwagon, closed land for the thrill of hunting and shooting. Woodlands and forests, where people had once scavenged for fuel and food, became no-go areas, preserved for game, such as pheasants and partridges, deer and wildfowl. A situation that the country writer W.H.Hudson called "the curse of the pheasant".

Barbaric Game Laws forbade the hunting of almost anything for food. Poachers – often desperate to feed their families - were treated with incredible harshness. Simply going into the woods for fuel for your fire could get you transported or imprisoned. Man traps and spring guns were set for interlopers, both having the potential to cripple and kill. River banks, where once people fished for food, were closed for the benefit of the sporting few.

Ancient rights of way were shut on the whim of landowners. "Come over this morning," one landowning magistrate would say to another, "and we'll close a right of way!" You can see the evidence of this on the ground to this day. The lines of what were once the people's highways still evident to the observant eye as you roam the great estates.

Even the highways of Britain became toll roads, adding to the profits of the wealthy. Toll bars and cottages were positioned at intervals where they could not easily be bypassed, so that turnpike trusts might gain payments from travellers. Toll keepers were generally unpopular with everyone who had not got a vested interest in the profits they raked in. They were often armed. The travelling poor would try to evade the tolls by making their way along alternative tracks. Better-off horsemen would sometimes leap the toll gates.

There was, of course, resistance to all of these restrictions.

The Tory poet William Wordsworth took direct action to break open a blocked right of way on the land of Sir John Wallace, when journeying to Lowther Castle for a dinner held in the poet's honour. During the meal, an apoplectic Sir John complained that his wall had been broken down and, if he ever found out who was responsible, he would get out his horsewhip. At which point, Wordsworth got to his feet, saying "I broke down your wall, Sir John. It was obstructing an ancient right of way, and I will do it again. I am a Tory but scratch me on the back deep enough and you will find the Whig in me yet".

A witness to Wordsworth's action stated that the poet attacked the obstructing wall "as if it were a living enemy".

Woodlands – Keep Out!

Britain's woodlands are the landscapes most denied to the people of our country, their glades the backdrop to many of the conflicts between landowners and the landless. On many rural walks you will encounter every permutation of *Keep Out* and *No Trespassing* signs, warning of dire consequences if you stray from the lane or path and attempt to enter these green havens.

It was not always so.

A couple of centuries ago, local inhabitants would wander quite freely through the greenwood, gathering nuts fallen from the trees and dead wood for their cottage fires.

The very principle of enclosure and restrictions of access to land, especially woodland set aside for game preservation, has been challenged from its very beginning. By the nineteenth century, an open war against exclusive ownership of the land had begun, fuelled partly by the need of the poor actually to survive, and the increasing use of rural areas for leisure pursuits.

Such was the scale of this predation upon property rights that by 1878 the country essayist Richard Jefferies described it from the landowners' view as 'a great grievance'. In an article for *The Livestock Journal,* Jefferies complained that

the value of property has enormously increased, but the legal protection in respect of trespass has not marched with the age…a fine of a shilling, after days of trouble with solicitors and witnesses, is simply a ridiculous remedy, not to mention the difficulty of identifying trespassers when time has elapsed. It is hardly too much to say, that a man with two or three pounds in his pocket to pay nominal damages and fines, might walk across a country just where he chose, provided he did not get too close to dwelling houses, and come within the charge of being on premises for an unlawful purpose. The alternative of proceeding for trespass in a superior court is so expensive, protracted, and uncertain, as to be practically inoperative, except when great questions of right are involved. The whole question of trespass, in short, demands the early and the serious consideration of Parliament.

Richard Jefferies had rather a bipolarised view of countryside access. As the son of a small farmer, and a journalist contributing to the Tory press, he might hold up his hands in horror at anything that smacked of socialism and an attack on property rights. But as a country-goer not unsympathetic to poaching and country walking, he could see the other side of the coin. He was to adopt a more radical outlook to social issues in the years before his premature death.

His earliest country books, *The Gamekeeper at Home* and *The Amateur Poacher,* examine, in a most interesting way, the frustrations caused by enclosure and game preservation. In *The Gamekeeper at Home*, woodland trespassers are listed with predatory animals, poachers and vermin as the gamekeeper's *enemies*, whether they are the local poor gathering nuts, firewood and branches to make walking sticks, or the newly-urbanised visitor out for a ramble

The keeper thinks that these trespassers grow more coarsely mischievous year by year. He can recollect when the wood in a measure was free and open, and, provided a man had not got a gun or was not suspected of poaching, he might roam pretty much at large; while the resident labouring people went to and fro by the nearest short cut they could find.

This gamekeeper, of Burderop Wood in Wiltshire, had unusual recollections in this case or was misleading Jefferies with an extremely biased viewpoint. Game was rigorously preserved in most southern woods throughout the nineteenth century and both poachers and walkers were severely discouraged. In his portrait of the gamekeeper, Jefferies tells us that he and his underlings would shake immature nuts off trees to daunt locals from entering the wood for nutting. And for all his words about the halcyon days of freer access, Jefferies records the presence of an ancient man trap in the keeper's cottage

In a dark corner there lies a singular-looking piece of mechanism, a relic of the older times, which when dragged into the light turns out to be a man trap. These terrible engines have long since been disused - being illegal, like spring-guns - and the rust has gathered thickly on the metal. But, old though it be, it still acts perfectly, and can be 'set' as well now as when in bygone days poachers and thieves used to prod the ground and the long grass, before they stepped in it, with a stick, for fear of mutilation.

The trap is almost precisely similar to the common rat trap or gin still employed to destroy vermin, but greatly exaggerated in size, so that if stood on end it reaches to the waist, or above. The jaws of this iron wolf are horrible to contemplate - rows of serrated projections, which fit into each other when closed, alternating with spikes a couple of inches long, like tusks. To set the trap you have to stand on the spring - the weight of a man is about sufficient to press it down; and, to avoid danger to the person preparing this little surprise, a band of iron can be pushed forward to hold the spring while the catch is put into position, and the machine itself is hidden among the bushes or covered with dead leaves. Now touch the pan with a stout walking stick - the jaws cut it in two in the twinkling of an eye. They seem to snap together with a vicious energy, powerful enough to break the bone of the leg; and assuredly no man ever got free whose foot was once caught by those terrible teeth.

A few years ago, I visited a manor house on the edge of Dartmoor and was shown just such a man trap, a vicious looking engine that could only have been intended to maim any poor unfortunate who got caught in its mighty jaws. For weeks afterwards, as I roamed unheeded around the estate's several hundred acres of woodland, the thought occurred to me that there might be other man traps, long since lost in the undergrowth surrounding its ancient oaks, but still set and waiting to crush the leg of a passing trespasser.

In the earlier years of the nineteenth century, every walk in the countryside must have been fraught with danger from such well-placed man traps and spring guns. The most likely victims of these 'terrible engines' were not the skilled local poacher, who would be wary and knowledgeable when entering the preserved park and its wooded coverts, but the naturalist on the lookout for specimens, the literary gentleman seeking inspiration, the early rambler and, most likely of all, the local labourer and his family, desperate for firewood, nuts and mushrooms.

The contemporary writer and social commentator Sydney Smith declared in the pages of *The Edinburgh Review* that "there is a sort of horror in thinking of a whole land filled with lurking engines of death…"

Even on my country walks from the 1960s onwards, it was not unusual to find warning signs threatening dire misfortune if you dared to stray off the road or public path. The favourite bore the *caveat* 'Beware of Snakes', often adding for good measure the telephone number of the local hospital. Other notices threatened that, if you trespassed, you would be 'prosecuted with the full force of the law' or that 'severe civil and criminal action would be taken against you'.

There were still spring guns in some of the game preserves, designed to go off if you knocked into a trip wire, albeit just to send off a warning shot to the landowner or keeper rather than putting a dose of lead into your leg as in times of old. I have never encountered any man traps, but there is some anecdotal evidence that a small minority of landowners were still setting them, or putting about the rumour that they were, well into the twentieth-century.

But the desire to roam is fundamental to human nature. There will always be a minority who will never accept that they may not go where they will. In his delightful book *The Amateur Poacher*, Richard Jefferies positively revels in the idea of trespass, albeit in the illicit pursuit of game. An examination of his many writings shows that he must have walked, with or without permission, through much of the countryside of Wiltshire and Sussex. He loathed any sort of work on his father's tiny farm and was never happier than when free to roam around the countryside. And for all his legitimate wanderings through Burderop Park in the company of its gamekeeper, there must have been illicit trespassing as well, prompting Burderop's owner to comment that young Jefferies was "not the sort of fellow you want hanging about in your coverts".

Both Burderop Wood and the fields around Jefferies' home at Coate were very near the growing Victorian railway town of Swindon. With the growth of industry, many workers, perhaps dispossessed agricultural labourers and their descendants, sought out the countryside in their limited leisure hours, coming into contact and conflict with the restrictions imposed by country landowners. Some of these expeditions would be in search of a rabbit or bird for the pot, perhaps a legacy of a more rural upbringing. But even amongst the working class, there was a growing interest in education and natural history. Country rambling was a form of liberation in itself.

Elizabeth Gaskell gets the feeling of this new working class leisure activity in her novel *Mary Barton*, when she writes of labourers near Manchester who "…deafened with noise of tongues and engines, may come to listen awhile to the delicious sounds of rural life." While in her novel she refers to workers following a footpath, many more would have roamed freely across the land, particularly in the vicinity of the growing Victorian towns and cities, adding to the conflict between the landed and the landless.

The rural poor who were hanging on to life in that same countryside struggled to survive, continuing - where they might - to use the woods and meadows as a source of food and materials for basic survival. But as increasing numbers of country and town dwellers sought out Britain's open spaces both for existence and pleasure, so landowners intensified their efforts to create no-go areas to keep these interlopers out of their private pleasure grounds. Whole villages found themselves cut off from ancient sources of supply, the countryside surrounding them effectively out of bounds.

The naturalist W.H. Hudson tells of a typical land conflict in his book *A Shepherd's Life*, relating how a Wiltshire woman, Grace Reed, took on the earls of Pembroke over the right to gather wood in the forests around Wilton

It will be readily understood that this right possessed by the people of two villages, both situated within a mile of the forest, has been a perpetual source of annoyance to the noble owners in modern times, since the strict preservation of game, especially of pheasants, has grown to be almost a religion to the landowners...about half a century or longer ago, the Pembroke of that time made the happy discovery...that there was nothing to show that the Barford people had any right to the dead wood. They had been graciously allowed to take it, as was the case all over the country at that time, and that was all. At once he issued an edict prohibiting the taking of dead wood from the forest by the villagers, and great as the loss was to them they acquiesced...not a man dared to disobey the prohibition or raise his voice against it.

Grace Reed then determined to oppose the mighty earl, and, accompanied by four other women of the village, went boldly to the wood and gathered their sticks and brought them home. They were summoned before the magistrates and fined and on their refusal to pay were sent to prison; but the very next day they were liberated and told that a mistake had been made, that the matter had been inquired into and it had been found that the people of Barford did really have the right they had exercised so long to take dead wood from the forest.

As a result of the action of these women the right has not been challenged since, and on my last visit to Barford...I saw three women coming down from

the forest with as much dead wood as they could carry on their heads and backs. But how near they came to losing their right!

A Woodland Trespass

Vast areas of woodland and forest are still out of bounds to country walkers. In the south of England is a forest of over three hundred acres, surrounded on three sides by the curve of a river, the fourth side edged by a busy main road. This oakwood was once a Chase, a hunting ground from Norman times, part of one of the great manorial estates of the county.

In ages past, the harsh laws that applied to many such hunting grounds, with mutilation, fines and imprisonment, applied to anyone caught transgressing these manor grounds. In Regency and Victorian times, the Chase was strictly preserved for shooting, no doubt with man traps and spring guns set to deter interlopers.

Yet even then there was recognition of the woodland's beauty. In the nineteenth-century, a landowner built carriage drives that contoured the hillsides, so that his friends and visitors might better see the exquisite views over the swirling waters of the river.

One guidebook author, writing in the years before the Great War, tells us that the then landowner opened up the carriage drives to the public on certain days of the week, showing at least some commitment to sharing such beauty with others. It is a dramatic landscape, the wooded hillside falling steeply from an Iron Age hill fort to the white waters of a mighty river; great rocky tors rising steeply both from the hillside and the river banks. There was once some industry here, for hidden deep in the undergrowth are the shafts and adits of ancient mine workings.

While the Chase is no longer preserved for game, some local people have a concession for occasional rough shooting, and a fisherman or two might be seen near to the little footbridge on summer evenings. For such a vast area there is a limited amount of wildlife, as much of it was cleared in earlier days. The empty badger setts speak volumes about the past ferocity of unenlightened gamekeepers towards Britain's native wildlife. The near-island status of the woodland has made natural re-colonization difficult, though some mammals have been put back over the past few years.

There is no absolute refusal of entry to the forest and river banks. The landowner is not opposed to limited access by written permission. But the general public is discouraged. There are few access points. High wire fences and locked gates greet the visitor in the area adjacent to the nearest public car park. The fast-flowing river is sufficient deterrent to all but the brave or foolhardy on three sides.

I'd not walked through the woodlands of the Chase for some years, until my trespass. I'd no plans to go there on that quiet Tuesday but, seeing the autumnal woods from the opposite hillside proved too great a temptation. I'd had a fraught meeting earlier in the day and felt the need to unwind in some wild place. There were not many cars on the road, so I climbed over the hedge bank and plunged into the cover of the wood. There were one or two nearby houses, but no one was about as I headed along the brow of the hill along one of the now overgrown Victorian carriage drives. This rutted trail bore little sign that anyone had been there recently; there were the hoof prints of horses and old boot marks, but no suggestion of fresher human tracks in its muddy ruts.

You get a strange feeling walking through great woodlands, knowing that although this is urbanised southern England, there is no one close at hand. A fall here could mean that you might not be found for days or even weeks. Although this should be a perilous sensation, it is not. It is comforting that there are such places where we can still be totally in thrall to nature in all its wildness, a far cry from the over-comfortable state in which most of us exist if not actually live.

Then, for the trespasser, is the contrary feeling that perhaps you are not alone. You search the trees and the undergrowth for watching eyes, and even though you sink into a mood of pure relaxation, your nerves are geared up to the possibility of ambush. You think of what you might say if you are challenged. Will you be aggressive or submissive? Will there be a moment of violence or just mutual embarrassment? You look for side paths so that you might slink away if you hear other footsteps, the crack of a dry twig, or someone's conversation. The true trespasser seeks avoidance and not confrontation, unless it be an occasion when you really want to make a political point.

Walking beneath the highest trees in the Chase is like progressing through the arches of some great cathedral. There is a stateliness about such trees, inducing a feeling of awe that there should be such wondrous creations on the face of the Earth. Even in an early autumn, there is a great deal of cover left, magnificent leaves of every shade of brown and russet, continually adding, in the gentle breeze, to the thick carpet of vegetation at your feet.

Even the wider tracks are hidden by lost leaves and sometimes obstructed by branches brought down in the year's gales.

As I strolled on, I came to a vast open space surrounded on all sides by the forest; the track I was following forcing a way alongside a tiny stream. There were roe deer grazing not far from the woodland edge, some feeding and others standing sentinel, regarding each area of the woodland boundary for threatening intruders.

I was walking with the prevailing wind at my back, but the depth of the trees and undergrowth disperse the air currents in all directions, giving no hint of my approach. I lay down alongside the roots of an oak and watched the deer for nearly an hour - a real privilege to see them in such a natural setting. I've watched deer in these woods before, not just the roe but red deer that have made the long journey from Exmoor. There are also the strange little muntjac with their noisy bark, introduced to the area by some past landowner.

I wondered how to progress on my journey without disturbing the deer, when the matter was taken out of my hands. First one, then another, then all the deer looked up. I knew why. A harsh crack of a snapped tree bough echoed up from the valley, followed by the crash of someone forcing their way uphill through the scrub. The outer branches of a holly shivered and a man emerged on to the track.

The deer had not waited for his appearance but disappeared into the forest on the opposite side of the clearing. I knew the man. He was an estate worker who had the occasional duty of patrolling the Chase in search of interlopers. He was quite elderly, with a ruddy face and grey hair straddling out from beneath an old tweed cap. He paused on the track, out of breath from the arduous climb up from the river and the fishermen's footbridge.

I considered at first that I might have been seen entering the Chase and the man sent over to find me, but decided it was pure coincidence that we were together in the woodland. He didn't seem to be searching for anyone, just enjoying a work day on his own, away from managerial eyes. I slid back away from the oak and backwards into deeper vegetation, keeping him in sight all the while. Just as well, as a moment later he turned down the track towards me. I watched as he passed within a few feet, obviously unaware of my presence, breathing heavily as he negotiated the fallen branches.

I sometimes wonder, when on a trespassing walk, whether I'm passing hidden watchers in exactly that same way. Woods are deep and secret places and your imagination hints that there might be a thousand hidden eyes. In olden times, when the Chase was a game preserve, both keeper and poacher would have been wary of being observed, watching the signs of nature for hints that they were not alone.

In well preserved woods, it's very difficult to move quietly at all. On a ramble in Sussex, I must have put up a hundred very noisy pheasants in the course of a couple of miles. There is the running of the deer, the sudden bolt of rabbit and hare, even an alarmed blackbird. All give warnings that there is someone about. In farm fields, cows often come to investigate the passing rambler. Sheep head away from the hillwalkers on moorland and mountain. Pigeons divert from their course as they pass near walkers. All draw the eyes and ears of those who would oppose the trespasser.

I could hear the man for nearly half an hour as he continued on his way. But I saw no more deer as I came out on to the track and set off in the opposite direction, downhill now towards the river. The path was steep and overgrown. It was hard to imagine the Victorian trippers negotiating it by horse and carriage. They must have had exciting expeditions. How often was their sightseeing observed by some unauthorised spectator?

I heard the river long before it came into view. For a while, the track contoured just above its banks for a long stretch, before making one final dip towards the lower carriage drive that followed its course. It had rained heavily in the previous weeks and the high moorland was issuing forth its stored moisture. White water broke over fierce rapids. Dark and jagged rocks, emerging from the thundering flow, seemed to tear apart the river itself. If anything else was making a noise in that landscape, it could not be heard against the roar of the river. A thousand watchers might yell disapproval at my presence, but they were as silence itself against the sounds that boiled through the valley.

A long length of almost pure white water led to a sudden curve in the river, where it fell into a deep and dark pool. On the opposite bank, a great cliff arose from the pool, rising high above the banks and the surrounding trees. Even in autumn, little sunlight penetrated to the black waters of this quieter stretch of river. The pool is famously deep but has a forbidding atmosphere that seems to deter the swimmer. It is a place just made for suicide. Its sinister waters seem to urge you to the very act of jumping. I once intended to spend an evening there watching for otters but felt so depressed I hurried away after just an hour. I stayed there on my trespass for only the briefest of moments before continuing back upstream.

The carriage drive brought me to the miniature suspension bridge used by fishermen. The gate was unlocked, so I crossed and left the privacy of the Chase behind.

I'd walked through one of the most magnificent landscapes in southern England. Seen once again spectacular and beautiful river scenery and tramped beneath tall and majestic trees. But how sad that this land, countryside that should be the common heritage of us all, is barred to those who might most delight in its wonders.

Forbidden Lands

If you want a symbol for much of the British countryside, then picture a strand of barbed wire, the ultimate 'Keep Out' sign. The Forbidden Lands are out there. It is time they were "Forbidden" no more.

Moorland: The gate was locked and strewn with barbed wire. Notices warned people to keep out, despite the fact that the track beyond had been an ancient right of way since time immemorial. A track of huge importance historically, one of the principal walking and riding routes in the Dartmoor National Park. The old route from Hexworthy to the long-deserted Hensroost Mine.

Who closed this lovely old path?

Step forward HRH The Prince of Wales (Prince Charles), his Duchy of Cornwall officials and various tenants.

Now Dartmoor, historically, never had restrictions on access to its open moorland and newtakes. It wasn't like the grouse moors of the north. *De facto* access was taken for granted. You walked where you liked. Generations of moorland landowners accepted this principle – until recent decades.

The rot set in with the closure of the Hensroost Mine Track in the 1980s. One day, the gates were fastened and the apparatus of Forbidden Britain – the barbed wire, the *No Trespassing* notices etc. – appeared. Anecdotal accounts related that walkers were thrown off the ground.

Attempts were made to gain the path as a definitive right of way. But legal technicalities – mostly His Royal Highness, and his immensely wealthy Duchy, pulling rank – scuppered any progress. There were High Court challenges. There were public inquiries. Nothing worked. The Hensroost Mine Track is still not a public right of way.

But now you can walk there!

The CRoW Act (*Countryside and Rights of Way Act 2000*) mapped the whole length of the track as moorland. Public access was restored. In 2005, I was privileged to be invited to lead the CRoW opening walk in Devon. After a great sweep across Holne Moor, my large party of walkers headed down the disputed mine track, opening the route for public access once again. Prince Charles has remained uncharacteristically silent on the whole issue.

Not that some of us had ever stopped walking there. Determined Dartmoor ramblers had continued to walk the track during the long years of closure. I made a point of walking the closed path about once a month.

Many of us have continued to walk other disputed areas of Dartmoor as well. Perhaps inspired by the Hensroost denial of access, other landowners closed land within the Dartmoor National Park.

Vixen Tor is the highest freestanding rock on Dartmoor. From certain angles it resembles the Sphinx. It's much beloved by walkers and rock-climbers. A while ago it acquired new owners. They promptly closed off the public access. Barbed wire and hideous *Keep Out* notices appeared. The tor is still closed to public access, though there have been any number of individual and mass trespasses by walkers and climbers. Because of a technicality, the CRoW Act failed to restore public access. Vixen Tor is one of a number of Dartmoor landmarks that may only be visited by the trespasser. So the trespassing will go on.

Downlands: Okay, let's face it, *the Countryside and Rights of Way Act* (CRoW) didn't work as far as England's downlands are concerned. What should have vastly improved the right to roam over the downs didn't work.

The idea of including downland in CroW was to restore ancient roaming rights to areas like the South and North Downs, the downlands of Wiltshire, Berkshire and so on. Had it worked, there would now be a right to roam over thousands of square miles of downland. Downland owners wriggled out of CroW, mostly on the grounds that the vast majority of downland had been "improved" (much the same argument used by the owner of Vixen Tor on Dartmoor).

This is, of course, a fatuous argument. Most of the British landscape has been improved in one way or another. Is that an excuse to keep the British public out? The same British public which, through taxation, puts loads of money into the pockets of these self-same landowners?

Now, huge areas of downland, such an inspiration to writers like Richard Jefferies, W.H. Hudson and Edward Thomas, are still officially barred to the public, scarred with hideous fencing, and at danger from further "improvement".

So what are we to do?

Amend CRoW to make the Act stronger?

I don't think so.

While I supported and campaigned for CRoW, given it was the only legislation around at the time, I was never in favour of such a partialist measure in itself. I've always believed that the people of Britain should have absolute freedom to roam. Surely what is good enough for the Scots is good enough for the people of England and Wales? So let us all campaign for that now. Let's get on with the job!

Coast: Surely the people of an island nation should have a basic right in law to access as much of their coastline as possible? And the British Parliament has agreed, bringing in to law, under the last Labour Government in 2009 the *Marine and Coastal Access Act*.

The South West Coast Path has been a huge success, bringing in walkers from all over the world. This coast path brings in over £300 million a year into often hard-pressed, coastal communities, supporting hundreds of businesses and jobs. The path is of hallmark quality, but it wasn't always so. I can remember there being a great many gaps in the path, filled in over the decades thanks to the sterling work of the Ramblers Association and the South West Coast Path Association.

It wasn't easy. There was quite a bit of landowner and political opposition. Many of the scare stories we are now hearing about wider public access were spread about. They were rubbished and common sense triumphed.

Every part of our country should have access as good as the South West Coast Path, or even better. Is that too much to ask? *The Marine and Coastal Access Act* should help.

Let us claim the coast!

Rivers and Waterways: The Scottish *Land Reform Act* gives full access to Scotland's rivers and waterways – and not just on foot. It also gives the right to swim and, where practicable, to canoe, kayak and boat. Sadly, the same doesn't apply to the rest of the British Isles. What a pity! There are few lovelier experiences than following a river to its source. Rivers have such personalities, whether they be the gentler waters of our lowlands that thread peacefully through our meadows or the fierce torrents of the uplands, the white waters that crash down through moorland and mountain. There are exceptions. It is now possible to walk virtually all of the River Thames on rights of way, but other rivers have paths only for short stretches. I've walked the lengths of many British rivers but have only been able to complete my journeys by trespassing. Yet ramblers cause as little disturbance, less probably, than anglers. Rivers are one of the most important geographical features of our landscape. Is it not time they were given back to us?

Trespassing In Scotland

The people of Scotland are fortunate to have some of the best free walking in Europe. *The Scottish Land Reform Act* of 2003 gives an almost unlimited right to roam to the Scottish countryside.

It was not always so! In the years following the Highland Clearances, great stretches of land were given over to sheep grazing and then deerstalking. Ramblers were discouraged. Tenants on some of the Highland Estates were warned that they would be evicted if they gave accommodation to walkers. Even in my time, it was not unusual to see signs in Scotland warning that you could be shot if you progressed across moor and mountain.

There were some memorable access battles in Scotland in Victorian times. Perhaps none more notorious than the clashes between the Duke of Atholl, he characteristically changed his title from the historic Athole, and walkers attempting to walk through the wild and dramatic Glen Tilt, the long glen that climbs between the Grampian Mountains from near the white-painted Blair Castle.

It was in Glen Tilt, a particularly scenic part of the Duke's 200,000 acres, that one of the most memorable of Victorian access battles took place. The track through Glen Tilt, the only direct route from Blair to Braemar and Deeside, had been a drovers' route for centuries and was much used by the growing number of recreational walkers, until the sixth duke began to forbid public access.

The first recorded conflict was in 1847, between the Duke and Professor John Hutton Balfour and a party of botanical students from Edinburgh University, who were forced off the ancient track.

Now, the presumption has always been that Balfour was just out for an innocent walk when he encountered the Duke. But it is likely that the professor was, in fact, deliberately testing the right to walk along the Glen Tilt track. Balfour was a trespasser and free-wanderer by nature.

Earlier on the same walking tour, he'd walked the Luibeg route up Ben Macdui in the Cairngorms, despite that way being forbidden by the landowner, the Earl of Fife, who had the route to the Ben's summit jealously guarded by his keepers. Balfour must have also known that, just a few weeks earlier, The Edinburgh Association for the Protection of Roadways in Scotland had declared their intention to campaign for the right to walk through Glen Tilt.

The professor and his students had set out from Braemar, observing the flora of the glen for some nine miles before they were challenged by a shooting party led by a Captain Oswald, a Captain Drummond and several ghillies and servants. The botanists were ordered to turn back to Braemar. They refused to do so and pointed out that the track was a public road. The walkers continued on their way until they encountered a locked gate at Tibby's Lodge, where a ghillie evidently summoned up the Duke, who seems to have gone into a rage at their presence

The Duke then said, "Well you must return; you don't move an inch further, unless you break open the gate, which you may do, and take the consequences. Don't spoil my walks with stamping. Come off that walk every one of you. Every step you take is a trespass - a new trespass. I shall not count it an additional trespass if you return on the main Walk." Professor Balfour - "Oh, it's a trespass then on the side walk, but not on the main walk." The Duke - "I shall not waste any more words with you; you must return."

Given that the passage through Glen Tilt is a considerable walking challenge, the trespassers refused to retreat back to Braemar, though they were forced off the track, as the press reported, and "in their desperation, they made their escape over a wall, hotly pursued by the Duke's familiars."

Unfortunately for Atholl, the case for access was taken up by the newly-created Edinburgh Society for the Preservation of Rights of Way, formed "for protecting the public against being robbed of its walks by private cunning and perseverance". Three of its members, Alex Torrie, an advocate, Robert Cox, a Writer to the Signet, and Charles Law, a merchant, brought an action against the Duke in the Edinburgh Court of Session.

They argued that the road had been metalled a hundred years before and was kept in repair by statute labour. When the decision went against the Duke, he appealed to the House of Lords, where he lost once again. While the case creaked through the Victorian legal system - mostly on Atholl's argument that its pursuers had no right to bring the action - the Duke made headlines once more over a conflict with two Cambridge University students, who found themselves accosted by him and his retainers as they attempted to use the old drove road on a summer's day in 1850. As one of the undergraduates told *The Times*

On Friday, August 30th, we shouldered our knapsacks and left Castletown of Braemar with the intention of walking to Blair Atholl through Glen Tilt, a distance of thirty miles. We might have gone by another road through Blairgowrie and Dunkeld, but as this road was upwards of sixty miles in length, and we were informed by all persons of whom we inquired at Braemar that though the Duke of Atholl, in spite of the decision of the Court of Session, was still endeavouring to stop all who made use of the bridle-road or footpath through Glen Tilt, yet he would not dare use violence if one insisted on a right of passage, we determined to take the shorter road.

It was a decision that was to bring them into conflict with the Duke himself, as one of the undergraduates recorded in his letter to *The Times*

"You must go back! Why didn't you stop sir?" (The Duke yelled). I again took out my pocket book, and preparing to write, said "What is your name?" "I am the Duke of Atholl" he replied, upon which we immediately tendered him our card (which he read and pocketed) and stated that we wished to proceed to Blair Atholl. However he insisted that we must "go back" to which we urged that the Court of Session had decided that there was a right of way through Glen Tilt, and, therefore we could not be stopped. He replied angrily "It is not a public way, it is my private drive! You shan't come down; the deer are coming, the deer are coming!" upon which we expressed our willingness to retire behind the lodge till his sport was ended, but he said we had been impertinent, we claimed it as a right, and we should not go down an inch.

Hereupon I said that in that case I certainly would go down, and if he stopped me it would be at his peril, upon which he became impatient, seized my companion by the collar of his coat, and attempted to force him back, refusing to listen to anything we had to say. This unseemly scene took place before the Duchess and another lady, for whose presence he had so little regard as to use oaths and other violence such as you would scarcely expect to hear from the lips of a gentleman. Finding his strength was of little avail, he shouted for help to his unwilling grooms, who were evidently enjoying the scene from a distance, and my companion, seeing opposition was useless against four men, allowed ourselves to be led away by a servant.

The students remained behind the lodge, being advised by a sympathetic highlander to wait around until dark and then sneak down to Blair Atholl. An attempt to escape up the brae was met by pursuit by two ghillies who at first threatened to take the students up as poachers, and then ordered them back to Braemar

They told us that we would be closely watched, and if we stirred from the path we would be prosecuted for trespassing. On parting, they took care to tell us that it was not their fault; and I will do them justice to say that they did their work very reluctantly. Well now, there was nothing to do but to take the old ghillies advice and wait till dark. The hills on each side were very steep, so that, besides the danger of being taken up for trespass, it would have been no easy matter to find our way to a village distant 10 miles. For four long hours, then, we were forced to walk up and down this bleak vale in order to ward off the chill autumn evening. When it became dark we proceeded on our way, which gave us no little trouble and uncertainty, as the darkness of the night was increased by the black shade of the pine forests. However, by midnight we reached the hotel, and soon recovered from the fatigue of a day, which, after all, gave us a good deal of amusement.

But this was not the end of the matter. Two days later *The Times* published a leader about the event. The editorial voice thundered

The public have as perfect a right of "way" through the Vale of Glen Tilt as the Duke of Atholl has to the possession of any acre of the property which constitutes his estate. The right in the one case, as the title in the other, is the mere creature of law.

In point of fact there was not, at that time, a ruling on the right of way itself, only on the right of the Edinburgh Society to bring the matter to law. However, the Duke appeared to lose interest in the quarrel, perhaps not least because his actions led to him being lampooned in the magazine *Punch* and criticised in the correspondence columns of *The Times*.

With the removal of much of the population of the Highlands and the replacement of traditional farming with the creation of sporting estates and deer forests, walkers were discouraged from entering some of the finest areas of the British Isles. Such prohibition coincided with the greater desire of

Victorians to explore the countryside and this put the freedom to roam on a wider political agenda.

The proprietors of the deer forests took considerable pains to keep walkers out. Pressure was brought upon crofters and tenants not to offer accommodation to walkers, inns were closed down, and rights of way summarily denied. Not long before those Cambridge undergraduates had dared to ramble down Glen Tilt, the Duke of Atholl had had a footbridge removed, so that the swirling Highland waters might act as a further obstruction against traditional access.

John Stuart Blackie, who would have known Professor Balfour well, was a great classicist, Professor of Greek at Edinburgh University, a radical and nationalist, who regularly championed the rights of the working class and fought against over-privileged landowners. He regularly free-wandered across the hills of Scotland, and in 1867 climbed the Buachaille Etive Mor – now one of the most photographed mountains in the world – against the express orders of its owner.

Arriving later in Fort William, he enjoyed drinks with an amused Procurator Fiscal, whom the owner had insisted should prosecute the professor. Unhindered by such legal threats, the professor returned to Edinburgh, where he regularly walked the streets in his stravaiging outfit of a plaid, worn shepherd-wise over one shoulder and under the other, complete with a broad-brimmed hat, carrying his big walking staff.

Not all opponents of access were so Establishment. The right to walk the ancient drovers' track from Glen Doll To Braemar, through Glen Clova, was won by the Scottish Rights of Way Society in 1888, following the stand taken by local shepherd Jock Winter, who fought for the right to roam against the landowner Duncan Macpherson, who had bought the Glen Doll estate and sought to ban people from walking across his land. The Society brought many old shepherds into court, all giving evidence of how they'd driven animals along the drovers' path over many years. His unwise actions led to Macpherson's bankruptcy.

The formation of the Scottish Rights of Way Society in 1845 led to many such legal actions that saved a number of ancient tracks, but the wider issue of preserving access to mountains and moorland was a battle that was to lumber on for generations, both in and out of Parliament.

The politician and diplomat James Bryce described the frustrations of these access restrictions in 1892

If, for instance, I was going to the top of a mountain, and saw in the distance the cliffs overhanging a loch, I am not to be prevented from going to that loch because it happens to be in a deer forest and off the footpath. That destroys all the sense of joyous freedom which constitutes the great part of the enjoyment of fine scenery.

These comments were made in a speech in the House of Commons, Bryce being not only a Member of Parliament but, at other times in his career, Professor of Civil Law at Oxford University, a member of the Cabinet in the Liberal Government and Britain's Ambassador to the United States. He was to have a political career that was rich in rewards, including the Order of Merit and a peerage.

But words were not enough for Bryce. From 1884 onwards, he and his brother Annan tabled several Bills that might give a legal right of access to Scotland's mountains. They were all to fail, despite having considerable cross-party support.

When Annan Bryce's *Access to Mountains Bill* was debated in the Commons in 1908, he received considerable support from the Tory Opposition and the blessing of the Liberal Government. A fervent supporter was the then Liberal MP Winston Churchill, (who attended land reform rallies, where he led the crowds in the song *God Made the Land for the People*). Ramsay MacDonald, for the Labour Party, told the House of Commons that he had often trespassed in Scottish deer forests. Sadly, the Bill was lost through lack of time.

Trespassing continued and the war on the ground became increasingly bitter. It was only in this century that the people of Scotland got the access legislation they deserved.

One of the first acts of the Labour Party in the new Scottish Parliament this century was to pass a Land Reform Act, giving the public access to all land in the country, with the provisos that one must not walk through growing crops or around the immediate policies of someone's house, the legal right to camp, and to use the rivers and lochs for swimming and boating. This was landmark legislation that England and Wales should have copied - but didn't.

Sadly, this much admired Scottish right is now being compromised by some Scottish politicians. Attempts have been made to restrict wild camping around Loch Lomond and elsewhere. The right to roam is still being resisted by some landowners. The present Scottish Government, and some local politicians, are ignoring these attacks on the *Land Reform Act*, favouring the influence of landowners and big business.

These restrictions must be vigorously resisted. The right to stravaig and free-wander must be preserved and the intentions of the *Land Reform Act* be vigorously upheld.

Access Battles in the Lake District

The Lake District is one of the great walking places of this country, visited by millions of tourists every year, many coming to walk. Unlike the Peak District, with its long history of walking restrictions and trespassing, some people believe there has always been free access. True, there haven't been many access battles or mass trespasses in the past century.

But there were fights for walking freedom in the Lakes, particularly in the Victorian era – civil disobedience and mass trespassing on as great a scale as the more famous Kinder Scout Trespass of 1932.

The fellwalkers of today, who enjoy walking across the mountains of the Lake District, owe a great deal to these Victorian campaigners and trespassers.

The Ranting of a Yellow Earl

In 1933, two walkers – W.L. Andrews and A.P. Maguire – wrote a charming book on the joys of rambling called *Wayside Pageant*. As authors sometimes do, they invited a famous person to write a preface to their publication, no doubt to boost sales.

Unfortunately, they asked the Rt. Hon. The Earl of Lonsdale KG GCVO, a member of the Lowther family who owned great stretches of the Lake District.

Lonsdale, who liked to bill himself as "England's Greatest Sporting Gentleman", was the master of a couple of hunts and a keen shooter of deer. He was nicknamed the Yellow Earl, because of his penchant for the colour. He donated the original Lonsdale Belts for boxing bouts and took a keen interest in horseracing.

Among his guests at Lowther Castle, near Penrith, was Kaiser Wilhelm II, who visited twice, just before the Great War. Kaiser Bill popped over from Germany to shoot in the deer forest close to The Nab, a Lakeland fell where Lonsdale restricted public access.

Lonsdale owned around 75,000 acres of land and made a great deal of money from the hard-working miners who slaved long hours in his Cumberland coal mines.

Andrews and Maguire no doubt hoped that, being a sporting gent, Lonsdale might write an encouraging note extolling the joys of our countryside.

What they got was a rant against ramblers and fellwalkers, whom Lonsdale accused of endless crimes and clearly didn't want anywhere near his deer forest. Lonsdale began by referring to an occasion when he'd been out in his deer forest, trying to finish off an animal wounded by one of his friends…

At about nine o'clock a party of hikers came along by the Fell at Angle Tarn, where I had put a gate, and a notice that it was a private forest and deer forest, and dangerous to hiking, and asking those walking from Ullswater to Mardale not to go to the left of this notice. About ten o'clock some half-dozen of them came up, broke the gate I had put up, broke the notice, and wrote on one piece of it – "We shall go where we damn well please."

… another day we were grouse-driving, and just in the middle of the drive a lot of hikers came right across and drove everything back. It was evening, and our last drive. When we ought to have got most of the birds, but the hikers went clean across the drive, although the keepers asked them not to go.

Also the amount of damage they do in breaking and destroying things on private ground is extraordinary, and at times they light fires that give endless trouble.

Lonsdale's rant stops dead at this point, as though the Yellow Earl had got so apoplectic he'd had to go and lie down. Full marks to Andrews and Maguire, for putting Lonsdale's note in their book as it stood, showing the attitude this sporting gent had for walkers in Lakeland – many of whom had probably fought for their country in the trenches not many years before, against Lonsdale's pal Kaiser Bill.

And no mention in Lonsdale's attack on hikers of the fact that the owners of grouse moors regularly set fire to their own land, to improve the heather to keep the grouse on them so they might be blasted out of the sky.

The celebrated guidebook writer A. Wainwright, in his book *The Far Eastern Fells of Lakeland*, wanting to include The Nab in his guide, admitted to trespassing there, deploring the Keep Out notices and barbed wire. He says he got away with it "because of his marked resemblance to an old stag."

The area around The Nab was forbidden ground until the beginning of this century when the Countryside and Rights of Way Act (CRoW) came into force. There is no evidence that walkers since have caused any disturbance to the deer which still roam the surrounding hills.

A Hot Dispute in Ambleside

"Of all the mean and wicked things a landlord can do, shutting up his footpath is the nastiest," John Ruskin

Stock Ghyll waterfall, above Ambleside, has been a popular Lake District visitor attraction since Victorian times, its white waters tumbling 70 feet over crags in a fine stretch of woodland. Today, walkers may wander freely there in the steps of our Victorian forebears.

But the public's very right to roam freely to see this grand sight of nature, without paying for the privilege, came under threat from 1877, when free access to the waterfall came to be denied.

In August of that year, the land surrounding the waterfall came up for auction, finally selling to a local businessman called Alan MacKereth for £1800. MacKereth began his ownership by blocking the entrance to the access footpath to the waterfall at both ends and introducing an access charge of threepence.

There was uproar in Ambleside with local people furious at this outrageous attempt to charge the public to see a spectacle that had always been free to view. A protest committee was immediately set up, chaired by Colonel Godfrey Rhodes, a nearby landowner. The secretary was Canon Hardwicke Drummond Rawnsley, future founder of the National Trust, access campaigner, and chronicler of Lake District life. It was the first of several notable access battles for Rawnsley.

MacKereth argued that the path had never been a public right of way, a point of view vigorously contested by local people who'd walked the path freely for generations.

The Stock Ghyll Footpath Committee gave notice that they intended to walk the disputed path and, on 21st September, Rhodes and two members of the Committee, accompanied by around two hundred locals, marched on the first gate. Rhodes had informed MacKereth that he intended to take direct action. And he did, ordering some accompanying workmen to cut through the locked gate. The assembly then marched past the falls along the footpath, cutting open the gate on the far side.

A livid MacKereth served a notice of trespass on Colonel Rhodes and his committee. Rawnsley immediately went on the counter-attack, issuing a circular publicising the access cause, putting out what we'd now call a press release and writing a sonnet about the dispute

...shall craven men allow Desire of pelf and individual greed
To bar the gate and ask a sordid fee,
To tax the wondering eye that comes to see,
Take mean advantage of a brother's need,
And claim a toll for Nature's public show?

Hard-hitting, for pelf means money earned in a dishonest way, stolen goods or booty.

English law grinds exceedingly slowly, and the trespass action against Rhodes and his committee didn't come to court until August 1879. The jury were undecided and came to no conclusion. Nobody could prove there had been a footpath dedication after 1842, but on the other hand, there was no proof *against* a dedication before that year.

Colonel Rhodes, meanwhile, on his own behalf, had been buying up land around and including the falls. Around the same time, a group of Ambleside residents bought the land owned by MacKereth for £2100, promising to gift free access to locals and visitors once the money had been repaid. The threepenny charge was reinstated, though Rawnsley tried to fund-raise by way of bazaars to clear the debt quickly.

This solution proved to be as bad as the original problem with MacKereth's original ownership, for those who wished to see the falls now had to negotiate not only the land purchased by the Ambleside residents, but also the acres purchased by Colonel Rhodes.

At first, Rhodes made no charge but by 1885, as the amount owed for the falls' purchase had not being paid off, instigated a one penny charge for people to view the falls. As the other owners' threepenny charge was being compromised by Rhodes' cheaper admission, they decided to open their stretch of the footpath for free. Seeing Rhodes as a poacher turned gamekeeper, they also instigated an action to prove that the path crossing Rhodes' land was also a public right of way.

The whole sorry mess dragged on for years. Eventually, thanks to land donations – including by Colonel Rhodes – free access to the Stock Ghyll was restored. Today, you may wander freely to see the waterfall, passing through the gates that were once part of the original problem.

Perhaps the most important legacy of the dispute was that it gave Canon Rawnsley his first blooding as an access campaigner. As we shall see, he put his experiences at Stock Ghyll to very good use in other footpath disputes in the Lake District.

The Keswick Mass Trespasses

Access to Stock Ghyll was but one of many Lakeland battles across the ever-popular Lake District. In 1886, the *Pall Mall Gazette* remarked that "Every year fresh roads leading to a hill, a lake, a waterfall, or other thing of beauty are barred with *'Notice! No Road This Way. Trespassers Will Be Prosecuted! By Order.*"

The newspaper pointed out that some twenty rights of Way around Windermere had been recently stopped up, and that a Keswick and District Footpath Preservation Association had been established, with Canon Rawnsley as its president. In point of fact, the association had been founded in 1856, but had become moribund. The energetic Rawnsley, now the vicar at nearby Crosthwaite, revived the ailing organisation.

The *Gazette's* editorial ire was spurred on by two notable footpath battles close to Keswick, where access was being denied to the heights of Latrigg Fell, and to where a footpath close to Derwent Water at Fawe Park had been stopped up by landowners.

Fawe Park Woods were described by the Victorian novelist, and Britain's first salaried female journalist, Mrs Lynn Linton as "the sweetest ever grown between the sun and the generous earth." Interestingly, when the path through Fawe Park Woods came into dispute, this now almost forgotten novelist supported the landowner in trying to keep people out!

The land was once owned by Waterloo veteran General Sir John George Woodford, who lived at Waterlily Bay, and who welcomed walkers on his land. As the *Pall Mall Gazette* remarked "he loved the people and the children of the people, and it was his delight to make and maintain for public use good roads to all the best view stations on his estate. In his time, and long before his time, the Fawe Park road had been public, and he jealously kept it so."

However by 1887, the estate had come into the possession of Mrs Spencer Bell who had a very different attitude to the presence of walkers and sightseers. At her instruction, her servants locked the gates, put up barricades and made it clear that the public were not welcome in the woods and lakeshore of Fawe Park.

Around the same time, Mr John James Spedding of Greta Bank, who controlled land on the other side of Keswick, and also happened to be the chairman of the local magistrates, barred access to Latrigg Fell, that dramatic outlier of the mighty Skiddaw, which dominates the little mountain town. The land was actually owned by his relative Miss Spedding, who – though she actually lived three hundred miles from Latrigg – complained walkers and riders would disturb her peace and quiet!

Representations were made by the footpath association to both landowners, but both the Bell and Spedding estates were adamant that they would continue to deny access. At a meeting of the Keswick and District Footpaths Preservation Association, a decision was made to remove the obstructions on both paths.

The association dutifully informed the solicitors for the two landowners that they intended to take direct action. On Tuesday August 31st 1887, the association and hordes of local people set out to storm the barricades – in the morning at Fawe Park and in the afternoon on Latrigg.

As the protestors marched through Keswick, they were cheered by the local inhabitants. Their first obstacle at Fawe Park was a gate interlaced with thorns and barbed wire, backed by a number of oak branches. Mrs Bell's servants were already *in situ*, and it wasn't long before the lady herself arrived.

The *Manchester Weekly Times* reported that

(Mrs Bell) expressed regret that among the trespassers were many whom she had thought were her friendly neighbours... Such proceedings would cause not only her but the resident gentry to leave the neighbourhood, and when they were gone no visitors or tourists of any account would come to the place.

This would ruin the railway and the hotel keepers and Keswick would be left in poverty and desolation.

Her belief that tourists only came to the Lake District to gawp at the landed gentry probably triggered a few grins in the crowd. As it happened, among the protestors were a great many hoteliers, local gentry and ordinary folk who wouldn't have taken such a threat very seriously.

Mr Fitzpatrick, on behalf of the protestors, replied that they had a painful duty to perform, that they were sorry to have to resort to direct action, and pointed out to Mrs Bell that she could always resort to the law courts if she thought she had a case. The thrilled journalist of the Manchester newspaper reported

Mr Fitzpatrick, then gave orders for the barriers to be removed, which was quickly done by a blacksmith who had been taken for the purpose, and the way having been cleared a charabanc was driven through with about ten occupants, other members of the association following on foot. Several other obstructions were removed as the party proceeded, and after the asserters of the public right had reached the other side of the hill, where the public road from Newlands to Borrowdale is reached, they returned by the same way they came. By this time the barriers had been replaced, and they had to be cleared away again.

This action was widely reported in newspapers across Britain, and subscriptions flooded in in support of the association, including donations from the Duke of Westminster and the Bishop of London – the latter was holidaying in the district at the time.

In the afternoon, the protestors turned their attention to the right of way up on to Latrigg. Originally, the association had tried to come to an accommodation with Spedding, suggesting that just a few members of the association's committee should walk the way on August 29th, promising to "endeavour to cause Mr Spedding as little annoyance as possible."

Spedding's solicitor asked that this token action be deferred, which was agreed, but Spedding used the interlude to take some direct action of his own. Local worthy Mr Henry Irwin Jenkinson, secretary and treasurer of the association, who now has his name emblazoned over the gateway into Fitz Park in Keswick, complained

How was this courtesy received? Advantage was taken of the delay conceded to build a barrier of rubbish and saturate it with coal-tar. This was made with the full knowledge that the committee had not made public announcement of their intention to go over the path, and of their design to avoid anything like a demonstration… the result was, as all know, that when the gentlemen arrived they had to force their way through a formidable barrier covered all over with tar – an ungentlemanly proceeding on the part of Mr Spedding, which called forth universal execration.

After these initial skirmishes, both Mr Spedding and Mrs Bell replaced the barricades, stating that the 'whole mass protest was all really the work of three or four agitators and that the public weren't interested at all.'

The Keswick and District Footpaths Preservation Association decided to pick up the gauntlet and challenge that nonsense with more mass demonstrations. On Wednesday September 28th, some five hundred people marched again on Fawe Park, and on October 1st around two thousand protestors marched to the top of Latrigg.

The Fawe Park protest started from Keswick Market Place. As the *Derby Daily Telegraph* reported

There were six heavily-laden charabancs and wagonnettes, but a large portion of the asserters of the public right went on foot to Derwentwater and crossed the lake in boats.

The protesters were met by Mrs Bell's solicitor who warned that they would be moving any barricade at their own risk. But Mr Jenkinson declared that they fully intended to assert their right to use the public road. Taking the responsibility upon himself, he gave orders for the removal of the obstruction. The crowd cheered as the carriages passed through, followed by those on foot. Several other obstructions were removed in the same way. The protestors then returned removing several gateposts which stood on the road and obstacles that had been replaced on the footpath. *The Pall Mall Gazette* humorously called the action 'The Capture of Mrs Bell's Barricades.'

A few days later, they set out to liberate the terrace road across the breast of Latrigg, and the zig-zag path to the summit known as Calvert's Road. Close to the entrance of Spedding's residence at Greta Bank, some 2000 people were already gathered, waiting for the arrival of the association's committee and a dozen labourers humorously styled the 'Crowbar Brigade'.

There were speeches by members of the footpath association's committee, with a rallying call by Jenkinson, who pointed out

The people had shown their earnestness in fighting the question of access to the mountain tops. Latrigg must be their watchword, and they must not rest satisfied till all their ancient rights had been conceded. It was their duty to protest in an earnest, orderly spirit before all England, and they must not submit to defeat, but continue the contest until success crowned their efforts.

The landowners dismissed the protestors as a 'mob of loafers', but, as Jenkinson pointed out in a letter to the *Leeds Mercury*, among the demonstrators were

... respectable, as orderly, as well dressed, and as fine a body of people as could be brought together in any part of Her Majesty's dominions. Amongst these so-called 'loafers' were to be found ministers of religion, doctors of long-established reputation, solicitors, a Member of the House of Commons, ladies and gentlemen (landowners themselves) and finally, a body of tradesmen and hotel-keepers as respectable as any to be found in the kingdom, and tourists from all the principal hotels. Surely these deserve a more respectful word than 'loafers'. Further, the conduct of the workmen present would have done honour to any community in the world. Policemen, who were there, said they never saw proceedings more orderly and peaceful. Not an ill word was spoken, not a blade of grass was stolen, and not a foot was trespassed away from the public road. Never did a group of people meet more as a family, and more exemplify that there is a groundwork of goodness at the bottom of all human nature. It is a libel to speak of such people so disrespectfully as has been done.

The wise Jenkinson recognised the implication of these Lake District closures for other hills across Britain

The people of Keswick, who were present at Fawe Park and Latrigg, are fighting the battle of all lovers of this beautiful district, this garden and playground of England. Instead of being slighted and sneered at, they ought

to have the respect, the thanks, and the help of everyone, for the Latrigg case will affect the right of ascent to almost every mountain in Great Britain.

It was at this point that Jenkinson wheeled out his star guest, the reforming Member of Parliament Samuel Plimsoll, devisor of the Plimsoll Line, regulating the safe draughts for ships. Plimsoll had already sent the association a message of support following the Fawe Park action, "Heartily thanks to…the Keswick Footpaths Association for maintaining public rights, so that the lads of the future may enjoy the same rights that I enjoyed forty years ago."

The Pall Mall Gazette was ecstatic in its coverage of Plimsoll's appearance. *Plimsoll To The Rescue*, its headline screamed, before the protest even took place

Mr Plimsoll, we are delighted to hear, has put on his armour once more… Mr Plimsoll on Saturday will witness the right of way to Latrigg asserted as satisfactorily as it already has been at Fawe Park… he is going, and the Footpaths Association is acting, not a moment too soon. It has not been sufficiently recognised in the past how much is involved in the derurualization of England. At the present day public opinion is becoming more alive to the imperative necessity of preserving every national playground and beauty patch that the growth of great cities has still left to us. The nation wants such things alike for its body and its mind. The doctors at the British Association and elsewhere have been proving to us the physical deterioration that purely urban conditions of life involve. It is even more certain that no intellectual health, no imaginative greatness, no artistic genius, are possible among people who have no hill country to walk over, no mountain glens to explore, no lake sides by which to linger… the landowner who puts up gates and bars must only be allowed to do so at his peril. That is the fundamental principle at stake in the struggle upon which the Keswick people are engaged.

Fighting words indeed, and Samuel Plimsoll came to Latrigg in a similar fighting mood, claiming that those there were not just fighting for the folk of Keswick, but for the people of England. He told the crowd that he'd first used the disputed way – "now found impudently barred against him" - forty years before on an ascent of Skiddaw, and that he had never forgotten the magnificent landscape he saw that day. He warned the crowd that

If the gentleman who lived under the hill was successful in his efforts to bar them out, the people in the south would tremble for their mountains. Boxhill would be threatened, and their friends in the north might find Roseberry Topping and the Cotswold, Mendip and Malvern Hills barred against them.

Plimsoll condemned Mrs Bell for her rude language about the protestors and Mr Spedding for his foul actions in tarring the gate to Latrigg. He pointed out that Latrigg had only been surrounded by walls by way of an Enclosure Act of 1810, and then only for the grazing of sheep. He praised other landowners who had shown a willingness to share their acres.

With Plimsoll and the committee members at their head, the two thousand protestors watched as a blacksmith cut the chain on the gate. There was no other obstruction until they reached the junction of the Skiddaw road, where the barriers had been re-erected on Calvert's Path. As *The Standard* reported

All were easily removed, and the vast concourse proceeded to the summit, where cheers were given for the leaders of the movement, for Mr Plimsoll, and for the Press. Before descending a gathering was made on the ridge overlooking Keswick, and cheers were given which were heard in the town. The National Anthem was sung, then more cheering was given, and the people hurried down, well satisfied with their afternoon's work.

But this was not the ending of the matter. Miss Spedding's gamekeeper, had complained that singing the National Anthem and *Rule Britannia* might disturb the grouse. This might have inspired Miss Spedding to issue writs against the footpath association, and the case came to court in Carlisle in July 1888.

The Spedding family insisted that the paths were there for their own private use, but some forty local people – including the son of the poet Robert Southey – came forward to prove that the public had used these ways for generations. The court finally settled the matter. It was agreed that Spooning Green Lane should be recognised as a public right of way, but that the Terrace should remain private.

A brass band welcomed the protestors when they arrived back in Keswick.

Despite the compromise solution, the actions of the protestors had an effect on other access-denying landowners across the Lake District. Areas that had been closed to the public were suddenly opened again, as landowners became wary of so much bad local publicity. And today, you may once again walk through the beautiful woodlands around Fawe Park and across the spectacular viewpoint that is Latrigg.

Ten Thousand Trespassers on Winter Hill

Will yo' come o' Sunday morning',
For a walk o'er Winter Hill.
Ten thousand went last Sunday,
But there's room for thousands still!

O the moors are rare and bonny,
And the heather's sweet and fine,
And the road across this hill top,
Is the public's – Yours and mine!

Winter Hill in Lancashire was the scene of a very large mass trespass in 1896, when over a thousand folk from Bolton took to its slopes in a demonstration, after Colonel Richard Henry Ainsworth of the Smithills Hall Estate tried to forbid public access, closing a track known as Coalpit Road in August of that year, so that he and his grouse shooting parties might not be disturbed. A week later, the protestors marched again up Winter Hill.

Ainsworth owned the local bleachworks and treated his workers like serfs. He had no sympathy for those men and women who wanted to use their precious few hours of leisure walking in the countryside.

Boltonians and visitors had always wandered freely over Winter Hill, but Ainsworth had other ideas. He erected the usual *Trespassers Will Be Prosecuted* signs – the infamous "wooden liars" as the great rambling campaigner Tom Stephenson was wont to call them – and hired heavies to keep people off the hill.

There was a public outcry, which led to an advertisement, paid for by the Social Democratic Foundation, appearing in the local newspaper, summoning the people of Bolton to come out on a protest the following Sunday, the 6th September 1896. The protest was organised by two local men, Solomon Partington and Joseph Shufflebotham.

A thousand protesters gathered that day in Bolton to hear the speeches, with Shufflebotham telling the crowd "We have met today to say to Messrs Ainsworth and Co that we, the people of England, have the right to pass through, and we will do so."

Thousands more joined in the action – led by a brass band - as the march proceeded up Halliwell Road out of the town for several miles towards

Winter Hill. Some ten thousand in all. Despite the presence of the police, a locked gate was swiftly removed. As the *Bolton Chronicle* reported "amid the lusty shouting of the crowd the gate was attacked by powerful hands.... With a ring of triumph the demonstrators rushed through on to the disputed territory."

There were further demonstrations on the following weekends, prompting Ainsworth to seek recourse in the courts. He issued writs against the leading trespassers and pursued an action for libel, bankrupting the trespass leaders. His court action was as much about crushing working people and their liberties as thwarting the freedom to roam.

But in the years that passed, there was a restoration of public rights of way and access up Coalpit Lane and across Winter Hill. Ainsworth's court victory was pyrrhic, because the protest drew the notice of the wider public to all of the out of bound land in the district. The working folk of Lancashire took to the hills in even greater numbers.

In the 1990s, as campaigners and politicians fought for better access legislation, culminating in the Countryside and Rights of Way Act (CroW), Bolton Member of Parliament David Crausby, mentioned the protest to environment minister Michael Meacher

the lesson of this story is that it does not matter how many people march over the moor – be it 10,000 or 100,000. Without a statutory right to roam, the rights of the privileged few will eventually take precedence over the majority. The law will continue the rights of the Colonel Ainsworths' of the world to shoot grouse along with a small party of their friends to be more important than the rights of millions to enjoy the countryside. That is why a statutory Right to Roam is essential.

Crausby's stirring words and Meacher's commitment to Right to Roam led to the reforming Act of Parliament. In 1996, a memorial to the Winter Hill protest was placed on Coalpit Lane. The Winter Hill ballad continues to be sung, and a play was written about the protest.

Two Poets and a Gamekeeper

Since then I've thrown away a chance to fight a gamekeeper;
And I less often trespass, and what I see and hear
Is mostly from the road or path by day: yet still I sing
  'Oh, 'tis my delight of a shiny night in the season of the year.'
        An Old Song (1) by Edward Thomas

Late November 1914: The Great War was just a few months old when there occurred a minor conflict between a gamekeeper and two men out for a country walk, not far from Dymock in rural Gloucestershire. Unlike the battles elsewhere in Europe, no blood was spilt, despite a firearm being brandished and threats being made.

The gamekeeper, as is the lot of most rural servants of that period, has been forgotten, though the people concerned called him Bott.

The two men challenged are known to this day, famous, their writings still much read and loved. One was the American poet Robert Frost and the other Edward Thomas, the English country writer, and soon to be very well known as one of the greatest of English rural poets.

The incident was to have a profound effect on both of their lives.

Robert Frost and his family were taking a long break in England when, in September of 1914, they settled at Leadington in Gloucestershire. A community of poets, now known as the Dymock Poets, lived nearby. Edward Thomas stayed in the area on visits to fellow poets such as Lascelles Abercrombie and Wilfred Gibson.

His friendship with Frost was growing, the American encouraging Thomas to break away from hack country writing, so that he might explore the possibilities of writing poetry. These matters were discussed on the long country walks they took together.

On just such a ramble – "a long and aimless walk" as Frost later described it - the two writers crossed the path of the gamekeeper. They had been walking through woodland preserves belonging to Lord Beauchamp, though the land was at the time leased to a chemical manufacturer from the Midlands called George Albright.

It is likely they were first challenged by the gamekeeper, as they walked through the heart of the woodlands. Frost seemed convinced that the keeper had been tracking the pair from the moment that they first entered the woodland – Bott had been "scowling in the hedges," he suggested later. The keeper may have thought they were poaching, mistaking their walking sticks for guns.

What happened on that first occasion is unclear. There is little doubt that harsh words were exchanged and threats made. They went one way and the keeper, anticipating their route, walked ahead of them.

As they emerged from the trees on to a country lane, they were confronted again by Bott, who aimed his shotgun at them in a threatening way, complaining of their trespass. He called Robert Frost a "damned cottager". As they backed away, Edward Thomas was scared and Robert Frost livid. They discussed the matter as they walked down the lane, Frost getting even more furious as they progressed.

As the two poets retreated, Thomas began to recover some of his lost courage, complaining to Frost that the gamekeeper had behaved appallingly and had a foul reputation in the district, being harsh on trespassers and local people who crossed his path. He probably told Frost that the keeper had no authority to challenge them on a public highway. After all, their friend Wilfred Gibson – and presumably his guests – had full permission from Albright to walk in the woods.

These thoughts must have spun around Frost's mind. The libertarian American held the English class-system in contempt anyway. He began to question their ignoble retreat from some rich man's lackey. The "damned cottager" insult rankled.

He would take action himself, he said. And Thomas could come with him to see that action. They turned round and walked back the way they had come. They didn't find the gamekeeper in the lane but managed to track him back to his cottage.

Frost hammered on the door.

When the gamekeeper answered, Frost told him that if he ever threatened them again, he would beat the hell out of him, and probably a lot more. Had the gamekeeper not reached back for his gun, it is quite possible that Frost might have dealt with the matter there and then. It is likely that, at this point, Edward Thomas's nerve failed him and, out of sympathy for him, Frost backed away.

Either that evening, or maybe the next morning, a police constable arrived with a summons at Frost's door with instructions to arrest the American. The constable, seemingly aware of the gamekeeper's reputation, decided to let the matter slide, but said that he would have to make a report to the landowner, though it is unclear whether he meant Lord Beauchamp or George Albright.

Frost turned to fellow poet Wilfred Gibson for help, but Gibson washed his hands of the matter. He hadn't got on with Gibson for a while, following a lukewarm review of some of Frost's poetry. Gibson seems to have been baffled at the American's inability to tug forelocks. Lascelles Abercrombie offered Frost more practical help, consulting Jack Haines, a solicitor in Gloucester, who happened to be a supporter of the Dymock poets.

There is no evidence that any legal action was taken against Frost, though there seems to have been some correspondence between the poets, Haines, and the landowner Albright for a few weeks. It is likely that the matter was dropped as tempers cooled. Rumour has it that Albright told the gamekeeper that he should enlist if he felt the need to work out his aggression on other people.

But the consequences of their clash with the gamekeeper continued to reverberate in the minds of both Robert Frost and Edward Thomas. Frost mentioned the incident on many occasions throughout his life, sometimes with a chuckle.

Edward Thomas seems to have been haunted by the experience, feeling that he bottled out, that he was shamed into cowardice in front of his friend. There have even been suggestions by some biographers that he sought to redeem himself, in his own eyes, by enlisting in the army and going off to war. He wrote about the incident in his poem *An Old Song*. The experience seems to have changed the whole nature of the way he walked in the countryside, as the verse I've quoted above indicates.

Robert Frost went on to live a long and distinguished life, becoming one of the greatest poets of the twentieth century. Edward Thomas was killed by an artillery shell on the opening day of the Battle of Arras, Easter 1917. His late flowering as a poet gave us some of the finest of English verse, with the countryside as its theme.

Delight on a Shiny Night

One night I walked only by the light of the stars, through woodland and across the rough fields of a moorland border. It was a trespassing walk, the thrill of being challenged adding to the other hazards of the dark. I wanted to feel how a poacher might have felt on such a night.

There was a landowner I'd fallen foul of before. A man who might have welcomed an encounter with me in the dark, with no witnesses. His lands seemed just the place to go, for I knew he patrolled at night. There had to be an element of risk. Now I accept that poachers traditionally poach to their 'delight on a shiny night', but I hadn't the patience to wait for the moon.

I climbed the country lane from the cottage, a quiet road with little traffic, leading right into the heart of the troublesome gentleman's land. A tough two mile climb. Despite the chill of the autumn night, I was sweating by the time I reached the top of the hill. I'd seen no one on the way and I thought I might reach his land undisturbed. It was not to be. Walking between the high hedges, I saw headlights sweep the valley woodlands, heard the grumble of a Landrover coming nearer.

For a moment, I felt trapped in that hollow way, for the banks were unclimbable. I knew there was a gate a hundred yards on and sprinted for it, throwing myself across the top bar just before the vehicle came into view.

Lying at the foot of the gate, I went unnoticed, though I was temporarily dazzled by the headlights. This was my adversary on his way back from the pub, no one else would travel that road so late at night. Watching the red tail lights retreating, I knew my night vision was ruined. I crouched inside the hedge for twenty minutes, waiting until I could see again.

A close shave, but what did it matter? I was on his land, where I'd planned to be. Such narrow escapes become joys in retrospect. Moreover, I was in the very field marked out for the start of my trespassing adventure.

But I could see nothing, despite the slow return of my night vision. I'd an awareness that the hedge to my left seemed a trifle darker than the open meadow to my right. Walking downhill with caution, I felt in front of me, for I knew the landowner had a habit of setting the foulest kinds of animal traps. I was wary of getting tangled up in one of them.

There was the faint evidence of stars between broken clouds, but little starlight to show me the way. Yet somehow, my eyes were beginning to pick out the features of the landscape, suggesting that night vision is an ability we all have, one that needs honing with constant use. I was no longer *feeling* my way down the edge of the field but heading confidently towards a gate at the bottom hedge that led into his woodlands.

I'd roamed that way in daylight and knew there was no obvious path through the trees. But they were mighty oaks set around picturesque woodland glades, and the going was not difficult, particularly as I knew that I must keep heading downhill.

This was real poacher's territory, used to this day for rough shooting. Just the place where a pheasant might be taken under the nose of a keeper. To my alarm, I disturbed three of the birds as I parted the boughs of a holly tree at the foot of the wood. They scampered down the meadow below, chuntering noisy complaints at my nocturnal presence.

In the valley far below, a dog barked from the farmyard. I crouched under the tree and waited. A light shone through a window and then went out again. The dog fell silent. After a few moments, I headed out on to his pastureland.

This was the most hazardous part of the journey, within sound of the farm. In daylight, I would have been in full view of its windows. The path contoured across the middle of the field, offering no cover. I fancied I could see the shady bulk of the farm buildings, but in truth, the valley bottom was one long trough of darkness.

I stood for a moment looking in its direction, contemplating the family that lived therein. There were several of them, but I'd only ever met the landowner, a red-faced individual who seemed to hate everyone, not least those who walked the place for pleasure. He was known to be handy with his fists, and with the great stick he carried when he didn't have his shotgun. His neighbours feared him, doing their best to keep out of his way. He shot everything that moved, patrolling his many acres at all hours of the day and night.

We'd only talked once, when he approached me in the village street. He'd objected to an article I'd written for the local paper and said that I "needed a good pasting".

I took that as the throwing down of a gauntlet, hence the trespass across his fields at night.

My contemplation of his psyche was almost my undoing. For so vividly was I reliving the encounter, that I didn't notice a feed trough across the path until I fell over it, measuring my length on the ground. Several dogs barked in the valley below. Lights appeared around the farmyard.

I ran into the next field, cursing silently, then diagonally uphill to the edge of the wood. I dived into the shelter of a ruined linhay, roofless to the sky, falling back against the granite wall. I gasped for breath, throat dry from the sudden exertion.

I've noticed before the overwhelming desire for drink at moments of physical crisis. I reached into my inner pocket and brought out a brandy flask, filled only with water. I poured half the contents down my throat and my breathing began to recover. It was enough. I felt refreshed and I began to enjoy the experience once more.

The dogs had stopped barking, the night seemed still. I peered round the doorway but could see no lights from the valley. I counted up to a hundred, watching and listening, but there were still no sounds or movement beyond the ruin. I left its shelter and walked the field boundary, ready at any moment to dive into the wood.

There were three fields to cross, all bordering the wood, before a gate led out on to the public road. I'd made my way through two before I heard footsteps coming in my direction.

If I'd been careless with the feed trough, then my adversary was even noisier. His boots kicked and crunched on the stones that had washed down from the wood. His breathing was heavier than mine. I crawled under the trees at the edge of the field and lay flat, turning my face away from the path. I knew if he had a dog with him I was lost, for no animal would pass me by. My luck was in - he was alone.

He passed within six feet of where I lay, gasping and muttering under his breath. I was helped by the fact he was travelling at great speed, no doubt thinking that if he hurried he might yet apprehend the trespassing villain. If I'd lingered in the linhay or by the feed trough, I'd have been caught.

Waiting until he was out of hearing, I made a dash across the final field, over the gate and into the lane. In case of pursuit, I didn't take the obvious route downhill, but climbed up through the woodland, then down into the valley by way of a little used public footpath. There was no light at all in the dense undergrowth. I'd to feel my way for great stretches of the path. Breath came more readily, for no one could outflank me without making a great deal of noise. There were great stretches of woodland offering concealment.

That was the end of my adventure in the dark, though aspects of my nocturnal journey would come into my mind when I read accounts of the old time poachers clashing with gamekeepers.

Our countryside at night is a strange world, a place of altered perspectives, somewhere we should all experience if we are to properly cherish the simple joys that make life worth living.

We'll Fight in the Hills

As I walked up from Hayfield in the Peak District, I thought of the crowd of young people who had headed the same way in 1932, intent on trespassing on the huge boggy heights of Kinder Scout. For it was on the vast acres of that northern grouse moor that a battle took place between walkers and landowners, the most iconic event in the history of rambling - the Kinder Scout Mass Trespass.

The moorlands above Hayfield and Edale are contiguous to the greatest centres of population in the north of England, being particularly close to the great cities of Manchester and Sheffield. They are vital areas of open space for people who work long and hard during the week. Perhaps even more so in the harsh industrial climate of the 1930s.

Sunday was a special day, a time for heading out from industrial grime, hard labour or the dole queue, to these bleak uplands, in search of recreation and fresh air. It was on these grouse moors of the north, that trespassing became confirmed as an overt political act.

Battles between landowners and the people were nothing new by the 1920s and 1930s. Attempts to close old tracks and even wider stretches of land had led to a number of battles in and out of the legal system. The Commons, Open Spaces and Footpaths Preservation Association had been founded in 1865 and was an early participant in the resistance against countryside denial - as it does today, as the oldest of our national conservation and access groups.

A number of other footpath preservation groups had been established during the nineteenth century, particularly in the vicinity of Britain's fast-growing towns and cities; in York as early as 1824 and Manchester in 1826.

Nor were these necessarily rebellious working class organisations. Archibald Prentice, in his fascinating book on the history of Manchester, describes the members of the Manchester Association for the Preservation of Ancient Footpaths as a mixture of 'Tories, Whigs and Radicals' who 'spread among the country gentlemen a wholesome terror of transgressing against the right of the poor to enjoy their own without anyone to make them afraid."

Many of the working class labourers who wished to avail themselves of the neighbouring countryside had that love of nature mentioned by Elizabeth Gaskell in her novel *Mary Barton*. With increased education and political empowerment, members of the working class began to look beyond the working week to their brief hours of leisure, the moorlands so close to the places of work being a great temptation and escape.

In the aftermath of the Great War, there was a strong feeling that the British people - many of whom had endured the horror of the Trenches - should be able to roam around the country they had fought for.

The philosopher C.E.M. Joad made no bones about it. He wrote in one of his many books: "I should regard it as a form of shirking, if I refrained from trespassing when private property lay in my path." Such incitement to walk across Forbidden Britain was not so unusual at the time. The journalist and tramping writer, Stephen Graham, could see little harm in trespassing adventures, remarking that "it is neither so wicked nor so dangerous to be a trespasser as might at first appear."

As we shall see, this was not necessarily the case. In some parts of Britain, trespassers – and ramblers generally - were becoming the victims of overt acts of violence. Conflict, danger and the venom of a biased legal process was not unusual. But as more people headed out into the countryside in the decades between the World Wars, there were fresh battles and memorable battlegrounds,

Rambling was no longer just the pursuit of the middle classes, the intellectuals and the literary. Even before the end of Queen Victoria's reign, rambling clubs for working and lower middle class walkers were becoming commonplace and walkers were regularly heading into disputed territories.

A typical example of one of these more democratic rambling clubs was the Sheffield Clarion Ramblers, founded by G.H.B. Ward in 1900. Ward was a remarkable individual, an autodidact and socialist. He saw the exploration of the outdoors as a way of restoring human sensitivity to workers who were effectively, just cogs in an unfeeling industrial machine. To him, rambling was not just a hobby but almost a religion, "a culture and a craft" as he recalled in later years

(It is) an intense love for one's own country, the innermost and the most remote parts of it, the sweetest as well as the wildest, a love for the wind and the rain, the snow and the frost, the hills and the vale, the widest open spaces and the choicest pastoral and arboreal retreats. It is a love for valley and moorsides, their history and their lore, which cannot be exhausted...

Ward suggests in that piece for the *Clarion Handbook* that rambling "compels a devotion and adoration which is equal to some men's religion." He certainly knew the northern moorlands very well and, having a desire to share his knowledge and love for the countryside with others, advertised in the *Clarion* newspaper for companions. A few *ad hoc* walks were organised and such was the demand that a committee was formed and the club established. There were some basic rules

The leader will take the ramble as printed - wet or fine. He has charge of the arrangements and will make provision for tea etc. but cannot be responsible for a large party. He should provide a reading or give useful information (place names etc.) from the S.C.R. booklets or other sources. Members should not defile moor or field with paper or orange peel or leave gates open.

Ward had great faith in the benefits of rambling on the human race. "A rambler made is a man improved," claimed the slogan on the handbooks of the Sheffield Clarion Ramblers. These booklets, often of many pages, began to detail Ward's explorations of the moorlands within reach of the northern cities, giving considerable historical and topographical detail.

These vast acres had been closed to walkers almost within living memory, first by enclosure and then game preservation, their heather miles being ideal for the shooting of grouse. The Clarion Ramblers' first walk had been around and not over Kinder Scout, access to that mighty height being denied by the landowners.

Even some of the footpaths that remained around these forbidden territories had only been restored to public access after hard-won legal fights by the various footpath preservation societies.

Ward often trespassed. His detailed accounts of moorland landscapes in the handbooks make it quite clear that access was often prohibited. Writing of the path from the Chequers Inn to Curbar, Ward remarks that "there is a demand for the removal of the alleged ban on the ancient and stiled path…it is difficult to believe how this path could have been put in jeopardy. I hope the new owner will have greater regard for this medieval right of way."

It is to his eternal credit that so many of these ancient routes were saved for future generations. This involved a great deal of hard work, poring over ancient records and meticulously searching out trackways on the ground. These activities led to occasional risk and conflict. On one occasion, when walking near to Woodhead, Ward was grabbed by the collar by a keeper who threatened to beat him with a stick. Only the intervention of other ramblers saved Ward from what might have been a severe assault.

In later years, Ward played a part in the access campaigns for a legal right to roam. It is perhaps appropriate that Sheffield's ramblers clubbed together to buy and present him with the summit of Lose Hill, as a thank you for his considerable endeavours. The modest Ward, in turn, presented the hill to the National Trust.

The 'Trespasser's Walk'

In 1927, the prolific journalist Stephen Graham, best known for his long tramps through Russia, thought up the idea of a "Trespasser's Walk"; whereby the countrygoer would follow a straight line across a rural area, negotiating all obstacles, human and otherwise, along the way. He laid out the basic instructions in a delightful little book entitled *The Gentle Art of Tramping*

You are going to be very ill-mannered and stray on to other people's property. Granted that fundamental impertinence you must be as nice as possible about it...

Graham suggested taking a compass bearing and walking the line through thick and thin, over every type of terrain that lay in the way. He warned that you might encounter fierce dogs, policemen or a "very peppery squire" who might assail you personally or set his keepers on you.

Such incitement to walk across forbidden Britain was not so unusual at the time. Trespass was regularly advocated by a number of prominent individuals, mostly literary and artistic gentlemen. Mainstream walking guides regularly suggested routes across land where access was questioned.

Having read Stephen Graham's book many times, I thought it might be interesting to see what might befall a modern day rambler who tried to walk in such a way.

To attempt his direct line trespasser's walk across open country - moor and mountain - would be too easy. So I set out for a part of East Anglia, where the barley barons had held sway for decades, grubbing out hedgerows and consigning other natural features to the rural history book.

Walking on a bearing, for any distance, across any part of the British countryside is easier said than done. It's particularly difficult to walk anything resembling a straight line in the enclosed lowlands. Graham admits this in the trespassing chapter of his book *The Gentle Art of Tramping:* "It is enough to do the walk roughly," he writes.

Fair enough, I thought. The agricultural district of England I'd chosen for my trespasser's walk was one notorious for resisting access on foot and which had a dearth of public rights of way.

I set out from a country crossroads, for the simple reason that a gate entered a field from the road and a track led vaguely along my south-westerly course. Beyond the wire fence, bordering the public highway, was a prairie field of such enormity that I couldn't see the other side. But the going was easy. The track might have been laid for me; it never once varied from my compass heading. Sadly, neither did the scenery vary - it was dire and boring. I began to contemplate a change of direction in the hope of finding more interesting vistas, but, after some deliberation, decided not to cheat.

At last - at long last - the track exited through a further gate in a barbed wire fence lined with an electric wire. It was here that I was first challenged. An agricultural labourer was stripping down a piece of machinery, cursing loudly as I approached. He looked up.

"Where you going then?"

I explained as briefly as possible, and asked if it was his land?

"No, it's all Farmer Blank's land. I only work for him. He'll flay you if he catches you - he hates walkers. He's a proper bastard."

"Doesn't sound as though you like him much?"

He grunted and tossed his head. "As far as I'm concerned all the walkers on Earth can come and trample here if it annoys the guvnor."

"Is he out and about today?"

"He's somewhere on the farm, so you watch out. He thrashed a couple of ramblers not so long ago. But he was well in drink and they did get a bit lippy. Anyroad, you won't get much further along the track there. It ends past the boundary."

I thanked him for his advice and walked on. The track stuck to my bearing, but the field was another huge prairie, partly seeded. As I journeyed across its great width, I wondered about the purpose of modern agriculture.

This was a sterile desert. There was no wildlife, no birds sang, and the increasing wind threatened to transform the farmland into a dustbowl. It was easy to see why. Every so often, a tiny ridge headed out across the field, indicating where a hedgerow had been removed. Such over-subsidised prairie farming has been an ecological and financial disaster in Britain, leading to the annihilation of flora and fauna across great swathes of our countryside.

About three quarters of the way across the field, the track came to an inexplicable dead stop, with not even a turn around for a tractor or any other farm machinery. But by this time, I could see a further fence and a gate, still roughly on my bearing, leading into the next field. This was narrower and, by some miracle, a hedge had survived on the far side. This proved to be quite an obstacle. It was thick and had not been tended for some years, probably in the hope that it might encourage birds and animals so the owner might indulge in a bit of rough shooting.

There was no easy way through the hedge, just a faint suggestion of a hole about half way up, where an ash tree had forced the brambles apart. I climbed the tree trunk and clambered through. It was a scratchy experience but, after several minutes of struggle, I fell out of the other side, sliding down a grassy bank into a sloping meadow.

This part of the farm had obviously not endured the prairie clearing of the first part of my journey. I could see why. Reeds indicated the marshy bank of a stream, a dozen feet across. It had been too wet to convert. I checked with my compass. My path led right across this water landscape. The mud was deep and glutinous, clutching at my boots and spattering my clothes. By comparison, the stream was easier to cross, offering a harder surface beneath its six inches of water. But the mud the other side was appalling. I scrambled up to the other edge of the field and sank down for a look at the map and a welcome drink.

This hedgerow had a number of gaps so there was no problem in going through. A greater difficulty lay in the presence of a number of farm buildings. A shoddy looking farmhouse lay directly across my bearing. A dog yapped in the distance. From somewhere came the far-away hum of machinery.

I braced myself and walked on. There was some luck in it. A gateway led into the farmyard and I could see another gate on the opposite side, not far off my route. The dog barked louder as the gate creaked open, but it made no appearance. I surmised it was probably tied up on the far side of the buildings. The yard was scarcely less muddy than the marshy field, adding to my general filthiness. I plodded across.

I thought for a moment I might get across without being spotted and I very nearly did. But as I drew level with the farmhouse, a figure appeared at the door, a tall and lanky woman, her hair tied up in a bun. She looked at me aghast, as well she might have. I must have been an unprepossessing sight, a Grendel crawling mud-stained out of the marshes. Her mouth opened. I smiled and waved and walked on. Her head moved slightly to one side. 'George?" she called in a quiet voice to someone back in the farmhouse.

Then louder: "George!" She moved back into the house, out of sight, with one last "GEORGE!" - almost a scream.

For about a second I considered lingering to meet George but reflected on the possibility that he was the violent Farmer Blank, so despised by his agricultural labourer. In any case, I'd hardly made a good impression on the lady of the house. I hurried through the gate, which led out on to the main entrance track to the farm. This curved away and my bearing took me through a gap in a wall and into a neighbouring field, probably just as well for within seconds there was angry shouting from the yard. I heard the gate creak open and the sound of footsteps running down the drive.

The bearing took me diagonally across the field to a narrow hedge bank that brought me out on to a byroad. A run up the opposite bank led into a tiny field and then into a stretch of woodland, where I steered a course between some mighty oaks, my compass held out in front as though the trees were a green mist.

And so they were, for I could see only a few yards in each direction, blind to any distant view. An occasional pheasant rushed into the undergrowth and a woodpecker tapped somewhere in the canopy above. It proved to be a substantial stretch of woodland, well-managed and full of wildlife, a treat after the sterile landscape a mile or so the other side of the road.

The wood was bordered by a track, which I couldn't follow as it ran east to west. My south-westerly course took me over a number of small hedge-lined fields, where a series of gates facilitated my passage. Every now and again there was a small spinney of trees to break up the landscape and one of the meadows had a decent sized pond in a corner. Here was a farmer working with wildlife. A few moments later I bumped into him, almost literally.

The gate had been locked and I clambered over at the hinges end. I staggered backwards and almost floored a slight man in a Norfolk Jacket and felt cap. He examined me through gold-rimmed spectacles, a look of surprise on his face. I apologised for startling him.

"That's all right," he replied. "I don't often see people in this field - the right of way is over in the far meadow."

I waved my compass and explained why I'd walked on a south-westerly bearing from the crossroads. A smile played on his face. "What? Across Farmer Blank's land? You believe in living dangerously, don't you?"

"It was on my bearing."

"I never mind walkers. Blank loathes them. I like a good tramp across the countryside myself. Who did you say this author was? Stephen Graham? Didn't he write a book about Russia?"

I explained that Stephen Graham had walked around much of the world and had been a prolific author. I told him about the Trespasser's Walk chapter in *The Gentle Art of Tramping*. He said that he must get it from the library. He held out a brandy flask: "Like a swig? Trespassing must be thirsty work?"

I'd exhausted the tea in my knapsack early in the day and was glad of this proffered hospitality. Trespassers are often tolerated but are seldom entertained and presented with alcohol.

"You are welcome here anytime. I believe in people being able to enjoy the countryside, as long as they don't frighten the wildlife and they shut the gates. Mind you, you've had the best of it. A couple more fields and you're at the main road and then the edge of the town. Anyway, must get off. Enjoy your walk. Must try this bearing walking. Sounds like fun." He waved a hand and strode off towards the smoking chimneys of a distant farmhouse.

As I arrived at the main road and sat on a milestone and munched chocolate, I reflected that a trespasser's walk of only half a dozen miles could say a great deal about modern farming and the attitudes of landowners towards public access. Walking on a bearing was an interesting way to investigate rural Britain. The Trespasser's Walk was an experiment worth repeating.

Sacred Land

There is no doubt that prehistoric man held the land to be sacred, in a way that's hard for us to comprehend in this busy, possession-obsessed twenty-first century.

Much of the British landscape is a palimpsest, one layer of a history visible, or not so visible, on another and another and so on. A glance at any sheet of an Ordnance Survey map will clearly demonstrate this, though sadly our mapmakers have removed many antiquities from their maps in recent editions. Scratch beneath the present surface of our countryside and you will find the story of our history.

These prehistoric and historic monuments, so rich across our land, are the common heritage of us all. But you wouldn't think so. For we are denied admittance to so many of them. What should be a right of access to our own history is often grudgingly given, charged for, or forbidden altogether.

Even Stonehenge, perhaps the greatest symbol of our archaeological past, is surrounded by ugly fences, with an exorbitant admission fee – despite the fact that it was given to the nation with the proviso that access should always be free. Much of the hugely important connecting archaeology, on surrounding Salisbury Plain, cannot be visited. It is permanently out of bounds in a military firing range.

I've a great interest in archaeology. I like to visit archaeological sites. But time after time, I've found myself trespassing to see some monuments. What is our common heritage has been effectively grabbed, taken over, absorbed into the private grounds of a few individuals.

A couple of country estates I know of, not many miles apart, have what are probably hill forts within their parks. On old Victorian maps they are quaintly called 'Danish Camps', though there is no evidence that the Danes had anything to do with them. No, they are Iron Age in origin.

Hill forts are a particular passion of mine. There was a time when archaeologists thought they were purely defensive. There's no doubt that some were used defensively, particularly in resistance to the Roman invasion under Vespasian. Signs of battle and skeletal evidence prove that.

But these mightily impressive monuments had a different purpose, or purposes. As meeting places, status symbols – imagine how impressive they must have been with stone and wooden ramparts, visible for miles across the countryside. Hill forts are probably the successors of the Neolithic causewayed enclosures, the first attempts to mark out stretches of the land. No one knows exactly the purpose of these enclosures, though there has been a great deal of archaeological speculation. Few remain and many of these are scarcely visible.

It staggers me that such huge monuments to our prehistory should have become the private possessions of the few. Admittedly, the two on the private estates, mentioned above, are not the best examples of hill forts. But they are important given their locations and for what they tell us about Iron Age territorial boundaries.

The first hill fort is hidden on the edge of woodland in a shooting preserve, its earthen banks surrounded by trees on three sides and a grassy field leading to heathland on another. For the trespasser, it's easy to visit. It is a place of wonder, an echo of a past and society that we can scarcely comprehend. I felt in awe of the place on my first boyhood visit, though the owner of the estate in those days was more amenable to the presence of walkers than the present custodian.

The second is within the parkland of a stately home. It's difficult to gain access. The last time I was there, the park gate in the very high boundary wall was heavily padlocked. I climbed the wall itself before making very visible progress across the park to the ramparts of the hill fort.

There are splendid views, right across the parkland to the grand house of the present owner, and the woodlands and countryside beyond. There were few signs that anyone visited on a regular basis. And yet, if the gate was left unlocked and a path provided, many might like to see this impressive remnant of the Iron Age.

These are just two examples of how our history and prehistory has been fenced away. How long will it be before we can enjoy the free access to the countryside enjoyed by our ancestors? The saddest words in archaeological guidebooks are "inclusion of a monument does not imply a right of access."

The Paths to Kinder Scout

There had been considerable public access on to Kinder Scout and its surrounding moorlands until well into the nineteenth century. But by the early decades of the following century, there was every chance that walking out on to these high hills might bring ramblers into conflict with keepers.

It was, of course, possible on occasion to seek written permission to head out on to Kinder. One of the owners, Mr James Watt, had printed on his permits the following

It has been my practice of late to allow members of the public, who asked for such permission, to walk over my portion of Kinder Scout, when I could do so without detriment of the ground as a grouse moor.

Were I, however, to accede habitually to the ever increasing number of such applications, the moor would lose its entire sporting value. The continual crossing of the ground is quite enough to make the grouse - a most shy bird - depart.

I trust, therefore, that those who apply will not think me unreasonable if on account of the breeding and shooting season, or for other reasons connected with the proper management of the ground, I am from time to time compelled to refuse the desired permission.

This was usually accompanied by a scribbled note from Watt giving applicants limited permission to wander on Kinder Scout on just one or two days.

James Watt was a poacher turned gamekeeper. In the 1890s, he had been an officer of the Hayfield and Kinder Scout Ancient Footpaths Association and took part in re-opening old tracks in that vicinity. Despite the occasional favour of giving written permissions, he seems to have had little sympathy with the desire of working people to roam on his moorlands. He used the deaths of two walkers, during winter storms in 1922, as an excuse to suspend all permits.

His keepers regularly chased ramblers from Kinder Scout, often with accompanying violence. There were occasional trespasses by the massed forces of several rambling groups who banded together for protection, managing to attain Kinder's boggy heights, but these were the exception rather than the rule.

Watt even came into legal dispute with the mild-mannered G.H.B. Ward, serving a writ on the veteran rambler to prevent him going on to the hill. In 1933, Watt placed a 'wanted poster' in the Manchester press, bearing photographs taken on Kinder Scout of several ramblers, promising a reward of £5 to be "paid for the name, address and occupation of any of the persons represented in the photos." Its appearance caused such an outcry that Watt never attempted such a tactic again.

Walking without trespassing in the Kinder district meant being corralled on to the very few available footpaths, causing the philosopher and ramblers' champion C.E.M. Joad to complain about being part of a human 'crocodile', a frustration to walkers who only wished to feel free after six days of hard work on the factory floors of industrial Manchester and other neighbouring cities: "Why (complained Joad) did we keep so religiously to the path as though we were ants on the run? Because to leave it was to brave an encounter with the keepers…"

Joad pointed out that in the 230 square miles of moorland between Manchester and Sheffield, there were only twelve public rights of way more than two miles long and that "of the 150,000-odd acres involved, only 1,212 acres are open to the public." Nor were private owners the only transgressors. Joad criticised the local authorities and water companies who denied ratepayers access to 39,000 acres of moorland.

A Sheffield rambler of the time, Phil Barnes, complained that "although Bleaklow is only sixteen miles in a straight line from the centres of Manchester and Sheffield, there are, surrounding this ridge, thirty-seven square miles of wild country, quite unknown except to a few ramblers who defy the unjust restrictions and take the access so far denied them by law."

Barnes mapped and photographed these forbidden lands, publishing at his own expense a book which became a starting point for those claiming that there should be increased public access. The idea of just being confined to paths was abhorrent to Barnes

No true hill lover wants to see more footpaths in the wild heart of the Peak, each nicely labelled with trim signposts and bordered by notices telling one not to stray. What he does want is the simple right to wander where fancy moves him - to seek the highest ridges, to scramble along the rocky sides of cloughs. In a wilderness of this sort a public footpath to which one is expected to stay is a restriction which offends, although the moor may not be fenced off with a physical barrier.

He was not alone in his quest. Mainstream rambling books, published in the 1930s, positively incited walkers to trespass, often giving full accounts of the wonderful territory that might be explored by the bold and adventurous. The popular walker and writer A.J. Brown wandered freely across the pre-War moorlands of Yorkshire, featuring his rambles in a succession of delightful books

I will confess (he wrote) that I am one of those rebels who believe that the moors and waste-lands are common-lands - much too vast and good for any one person to keep exclusively to himself - path or no path. Trespassers "will be prosecuted" (Perhaps). - All Yorkshiremen are "trespassers" (of sorts) at heart, and it will be a bad day for the country when they lose their native independence and instinctive resistance to any sort of encroachment on their natural rights.

During those troublous decades of the 'twenties and 'thirties, an annual rally for access was held at Winnats Pass in Derbyshire. These were well attended occasions with renowned commentators such as Professor Joad and G.H.B. Ward. In his later years, Joad recalled the atmosphere of addressing thousands of ramblers in the declivity of Winnats

Looking down from the great boulder from which the speakers address the audience, one surveys a great sea of bare knees and brown faces, studded with occasional islands of piled rucksacks and camping kit.

After each rally, the great and the good of the rambling movement would go away to negotiate and campaign with landowning interests and the powers that be. Usually to no effect whatsoever. As time went on with nothing achieved, Joad noticed a growing impatience and militancy among some of the walkers and a growing tendency to heckle those speakers who urged caution and diplomacy

"Here," said the militants in effect to the official speakers, "have you been urging these twenty years past that mountains and moorlands and waste places should be made available for walkers...you have voiced your claims,

and not only has nobody taken the slightest notice of you, but today more of England is preserved and closed to walkers than when your agitation began twenty-five years ago. Is it not time to try other methods? We think that it is. Yet when we try them you give us no support and continue to bleat your impeccable platitudes about making England a land safe for its citizens to walk in, in the wholly mistaken belief that someone in authority will one day listen to you."

Joad wrote this summary of heckling objection in the mid 'thirties, in the wake of events which had taken place on the slopes of Kinder Scout in 1932. The 'other method' referred to was a direct action against access restrictions in the form of notorious and, in time, mythic mass trespasses by moorland walkers.

Trespassing on the Great Estates

Huge areas of the British countryside are owned by relatively few people. You don't have to travel very far across our land to see the great estates, with their parklands, lodges, workers' cottages, often forbiddingly high boundary walls and – very usually – *Private: Keep Out* notices. Attached to the rolling parks is usually woodland, reserved for shooting. The places where man traps and spring guns were put down for the poacher and trespasser, not that long ago in history.

The houses range through many periods of British history. Many are architectural gems, designed by some of our greatest architects. The grounds were often laid out by famous designers, such as Lancelot 'Capability' Brown. Very often, whole villages were moved, so that the owners would not have to gaze at the homes of the peasants. Some of these estates are quite massive in size, as you can tell when you walk the perimeters of their boundary walls, though there are other estates, more modest by comparison.

These estates are the echo of the post Norman Conquest redistribution of the land. They were originally, and often still are, the rural homes of the aristocracy and landed country gentlemen. Very often, these days, they are the country piles of the *nouveau riche*; wealthy businessmen and bankers, pop stars and politicians. With few exceptions, access is severely discouraged.

The new owners tend to be even more rabidly anti-access than their predecessors. Having joined the landowning elite, they try to keep everyone else away; often their first act on taking possession is to try and close the nearest footpaths and bridleways. Closed circuit television has replaced the man trap and the spring gun as a method of deterring intruders.

Some of these great estate properties have come into the possession of the National Trust, so at least you have a chance to look if you are prepared to be a member or pay an admission charge. Even in private hands, you can often visit if you pay.

But, strangely, even the National Trust often restricts access to the parklands and woodlands to the casual walker, except where there are existing rights of way, ignoring the intentions of their founders. Access to the private estates isn't usually even that generous.

Yet these estates, rather like British farming, receive massive subsidies from government (i.e. the landless rest of us who pay the taxes that fund all of the bills). Some landowners receive the equivalent of a decent-sized lottery win in taxpayer funded subsidies each and every year. And at a time when the welfare budget for Britain's poorest is being cut to less than survival levels.

Given that situation, perhaps they should feel a moral obligation to let their paymasters in? Forget it! You can count the landowners who do on very few fingers.

As a trespasser, I've often made a point of exploring these great estates, the parklands as well as the woodlands.

The first I ever encountered was quite a minor country estate, with a modest house. It didn't have a park, but lots of meadows and woodlands, fringing the edges of a pleasant stretch of moorland. I knew it first when I was a youth. The owner was a retired army officer, a veteran of the Great War. He was a pleasant chap. I liked him. He was the best sort of old-fashioned countryman.

I first met him when I was walking deep in his coverts, seeking out a pond that was marked on the map. I expected the usual "get off my land!" I didn't get it. Instead, there was a friendly greeting. He seemed almost thrilled that I was there, asking what wildlife I'd seen and where I was going next. He told me he welcomed people walking on the land. He seemed sad that few did. In the years that followed, I often encountered him when I walked in the area. He would recommend places where I might see a deer or a rare bird. His mind often harked back to the trenches of the Western Front. I was pleased he'd found a kind of peace in those lovely woodlands.

After his death, the whole scenario changed. His son was a countryman of the new school. Gates were locked. 'Private' notices appeared. The estate woodlands were used more for shooting and – heaven help us! – *paintballing* by a new rich clientele. I suspect the wildlife decreased in the wake of these noisier pursuits.

Harry Hopkins concludes his scholarly history of poaching, *The Long Affray*, by suggesting that the rambler has replaced the poacher as the demon enemy of the country landowner and his gamekeeper. It is a shrewd conclusion. As poaching declined, rambling increased. Over the past century, the rambler has been treated with much the same venom as the peasant poacher, trespassing to feed his family. I've even had a gamekeeper suggest to me that *most* ramblers use country walking as a front, so that they might snig a salmon or take a pheasant. The suggestion is ludicrous. The majority of ramblers (surely *en masse* the most innocent of creatures) wouldn't begin to know how.

But I've walked a number of estates so heavily keepered that a country walk as such would be impossible. Trespassing every yard of the way, studying every bush for that hidden gamekeeper, watching for the trip wire that might trigger a spring gun. Oh, yes, there are still spring guns in our countryside, though the number has declined since I was young.

The original spring guns were of the nature of man traps. The trespasser tripped a wire, firing the gun. A dose of lead shot, or sometimes a metal bar would hit the intruder. Very often the spring gun would have trip wires going in every direction. Catching a wire would swivel the gun towards you, firing the shot as it lined up on where you were. People were killed or maimed on a regular basis. In recent times, these guns were adapted to just fire a warning shot if you caught the trip wire, warning the keeper that you were in the locality. Some country estates still use them.

Not far from the estate I mentioned earlier, is another. A house, a small park and lots of woodlands, just a mile or two inland from a bustling seaside town. Not that residents or visitors can enjoy its sylvan beauties. Rights of way are non-existent, though a country lane rises steeply between the pheasant coverts. The owners have tried their best to keep people out. Wanderers up the lane will find plenty of locked gates, fences, high banks and warning notices.

I can remember even now, my first boyhood expedition up that lane. It was a dark stormy afternoon, the light scarcely penetrating the road, hidden as it was with the branches of the trees forming a tunnel overhead. In those days, near to the foot of the lane, you passed several estate workers' cottages, including a lodge and the home of the gamekeeper. Even though I was on a public highway, the workers glowered at me as though I'd no right to be there. At the crest of the hill, I emerged on to open heathland. Looking back across the valley, I could see this vast swathe of forest, all forbidden territory, but terribly inviting.

I went in on a summer's evening, avoiding the estate cottages by taking a circuitous route across the heathlands to the north. The wooded coverts merged with the heather, and there were none of the access obstructions that lined the public highway.

After a few minutes' quiet listening, I slipped between the trees on what was clearly a well-used path. Too well-used perhaps. Just a hundred yards in, I saw the wire of the spring gun a yard in front of me, at about knee height. I trailed the wire back to the gun itself.

A warning spring gun, not one of the more deadly historical ones. Wires led from it in several directions. A careless trespasser coming in from the north could very easily trip off a shot. I wondered how long it would take the keeper to get there if I pulled the wire? His cottage was a good half mile away. Did he rush to the location of his spring gun every time it went off? He had to, if there was any point in having it there at all. And yet, the wire might be tripped by anything, a fox, badger, deer…

Now the devil was in me that night. And I'd never heard a spring gun go off. So I pulled the wire, before hurriedly making my way deeper into the covert. I must say it made a hell of a bang, far louder than I was expecting. The echo reverberated around the woodlands for several seconds. The very air around me seemed to vibrate. I crawled deeper under a holly bush and waited for events to unfold.

At first, I thought nothing was going to happen at all. There seemed to be no reaction. I decided to give it a half hour. It was as well I did, for it took the keeper and a dozen estate workers about twenty-seven minutes to get there. I could hear their heavy breathing and gasps as they struggled up the steep slope to the narrow path where the gun lay.

I could not hear exactly what they said, but there was evidently some debate as to what might have tripped the gun. They walked up the path to the edge of the heathland and had a good look around, but seemed satisfied that nobody was about in that direction. Then I heard the keeper bark an order and they strung out along the top of the wood, each one a few yards apart, like beaters on a pheasant shoot.

I'd not anticipated there being more than a couple of them. Had I considered there might be, I'd have gone further away from the gun. As it was, they could not help putting me to flight like a game bird. If I stayed under the holly, I would be scooped up by the middle of their line. Fortunately, there were no dogs.

At the time I was young and fit and something of a cross country runner, so I decided to make a break for it while I still had some headway. They almost view hallooed at the sight of me, crashing through the undergrowth in my wake. One of them triggered another spring gun, the explosion crashing through the trees as a loud accompaniment to the chase.

I'm always amused when I see people being chased through woodlands in films. They always go crashing on, the sheer noise telling the pursuers which way they've gone. They usually run in a straight line, often along a very visible track.

Now that isn't how you do it at all.

Unless you are a pretty fit sprinter, you are bound to get caught. In these days of mobile phones and walkie-talkies, you'll probably get headed off anyway, as the chasers call up reinforcements.

No! The secret is to get just off the immediate line of the chase and go to ground. Hidden away, they can't see you and they can't hear you. I've been chased through woodlands on several occasions and this strategy has always worked. On one joyful occasion, I climbed a tree, smiling as the hunt passed right beneath me. Experienced gamekeepers and countrymen may look up – their enthusiastic back-up seldom does.

The only danger is if those chasing you have a dog with them. Dogs can scent across incredible distances. Better to keep running, perhaps in the direction of a public highway, where you can look surprised when challenged, pretending to be a rambler or a birdwatcher.

Out of sight for a minute of two, I ran at right angles to the chase and dived into a clump of rhododendron bushes. The tactic was my salvation. A minute later I heard the hunters crash down through the wood a couple of hundred yards away. I waited until the noises died away and made my way back up to the top of the wood.

Experience has taught me that it's usually better to retrace your course in such circumstances, away from the direction of the chase. But you must always be careful. A tactic used by the other side is to position a watcher at the original spot of interception. Fortunately, that time, they hadn't thought of it.

This was just the first of many pleasant rambles undertaken across that woodland estate, though none of the others were quite so dramatic. On subsequent occasions, I found other spring guns, but resisted the temptation to trip the wires. Perhaps one day, local people and seaside visitors will have the opportunity to walk freely in these woods.

Country landowners and gamekeepers will say they keep people out of these wooded preserves to avoid disturbance to pheasants and other wildlife. That argument is a load of baloney. Anyone who walks in the countryside knows how reluctantly pheasants move out of the way on foot, let alone take to the skies, even when you almost tread on them.

Wildlife may move a little way away from a passing walker, but the movement is but temporary. You are just a passing blip on their scene. And, after all, quite large shooting parties and fox hunts bash through these same woodlands. Can anyone seriously argue that they cause less disturbance than a solitary country walker or even a modest rambling group?

The Kinder Scout Mass Trespass

By the 1930s, a state of near war existed between the ramblers on the northern moorlands and the grouse-shooting landowners and their keepers. Proposals for access legislation were going nowhere.

An *Access to Mountains Act* went through Parliament in 1939, but it made the situation considerably worse; with clauses that actually reduced access and in some cases, criminalised trespass. It was rightly done away with soon after World War Two.

Ramblers who strayed away from footpaths were frequently challenged and often quite viciously assaulted. Wanted posters appeared with photographs of trespassing hillwalkers, offering a reward for their 'names, addresses and occupations'.

Things had to come to a head.

Step forward a 20-year-old unemployed motor mechanic from Manchester, Bernard 'Benny' Rothman, rambler, cyclist, and voluntary official of the British Workers Sports Federation (BWSF).

At a weekend camp, members of the BWSF were turned back by keepers at Yellowslacks in the Peak District. Back at their camp, the members debated the injustice of it all. They came to the conclusion that had there been many more ramblers, the keepers wouldn't have been able to hold them at bay.

And so was born the idea for the most celebrated event in rambling and trespassing history – the Kinder Scout Mass Trespass. An event that has become iconic in our social history - Sunday April 24th 1932 is a date that deserves to be annually remembered.

The target for the planned mass trespass was the bulky height of Kinder Scout itself, one of the most denied grouse moors.

As the *Manchester Evening News* headlined just before the event: *Claims to free access – Campaign to Force Landowners – Call to Rally – Sunday's Attack on Kinder*. In the story that followed, the newspaper stated the objectives of the protest: *Tired of unproductive protests and pleas, working class rambling clubs in Lancashire have decided upon direct action to enforce their claims for access to beauty spots in the countryside.*

Benny Rothman told the newspaper

We are willing no longer to be deprived of the beauties of the country for the convenience of the landowners. It is our declared intention to trespass en masse everywhere where we can claim with justice to have a right to go. And Sunday will be but the opening of our campaign.

In leaflets circulated before the trespass, the point was made: "Is it a crime for workers to put their feet where Lord Big Bug, and Lady Little Flea do their annual shooting?"

Predictably and stupidly, the Manchester Ramblers Federation condemned the action, though that didn't stop many of their members joining in. The rambling 'Establishment' tends to be Johnny-come-latelies where direct action is concerned.

The landowners were making their own preparations. Much of the land on Kinder belonged to the Duke of Devonshire. His estate took on extra help to combat the trespassers; lots of gamekeepers, perhaps as many as sixty, all armed with heavy sticks.

They had the comfort of knowing that they had the backing of the police. It has been estimated that thirty uniformed bobbies were sent out on the day, along with an undefined number of plain clothes policemen, including Superintendent Garrow, Deputy Chief Constable of Derbyshire. By the middle of the day, perhaps a third of Derbyshire's constabulary were stationed around Hayfield, with reserves billeted in the local cinema.

Benny Rothman, who had done more than anyone to spread word of the Trespass, became the prime target of police activity. The police tried and failed to serve an injunction. They attempted to ambush Benny at the railway station but failed because Benny and his pal Woolfie Winnick travelled to Hayfield by bicycle. After a very English cup of tea in a tea shop, Benny and Woolfie surveyed a route for the Trespass, noting the presence of a large number of gamekeepers on the skyline.

At 2 o'clock, up to 600 trespassers set out from Hayfield, marching swiftly to outdistance the police, and singing revolutionary songs. In a disused quarry, Benny addressed the assembled trespassers.

To tremendous applause, he outlined the history of the enclosures, told them how the land had been stolen from ordinary people, and pointed out that alternative campaigning had got them nowhere. To the sound of a whistle, rather like troops going over the top from the trenches in the Great

War, they all set out for Kinder Scout. A group of ramblers circled Benny to prevent the police dashing in to arrest him.

Among the trespassers that day were the future historian A.J.P. Taylor, the Trespassers' press officer Jimmy Miller, who was to find fame as the songwriter Ewan MacColl, and the future composer Michael (later Sir Michael) Tippett. MacColl was to immortalise these moorland battles in his famous song *The Manchester Rambler*, the anthem of ramblers and trespassers to this day.

The Trespassers met the gamekeepers on the side of William Clough. Predictably, the keepers blustered and threatened. Then they laid into the ramblers with their heavy sticks. But Benny Rothman's tactics worked. The gamekeepers were outnumbered by the ramblers and were soon disarmed. One keeper injured his ankle in a fall but was able to walk down off the hill.

By this time, the Manchester ramblers were joined by a contingent of Trespassers from Sheffield, who had walked over from Edale. Benny made another speech and – in very British fashion –they all had tea. The two groups then marched back respectively to Hayfield and Edale, keeping together.

As Benny wrote afterwards, *"It was a demonstration for the rights of ordinary people to walk on land stolen from them in earlier times."*

Retribution awaited the Trespassers in Hayfield. The police walked through the assembled ranks and arrested six ramblers: Benny Rothman, John Anderson, Judd Clynes, Harry Mendell, David Nussbaum and Arthur 'Tona' Gillett.

They were charged the next day, at New Mills police court, with unlawful (later riotous) assembly and breach of the peace. They were committed for trial at Derby Assizes. Incredibly, Anderson was charged with injuring the keeper who had twisted his ankle.

The jury at the Assize consisted of two Brigadier-Generals, three Colonels, two Majors, three Captains, two Aldermen, all of them country gentlemen. Hardly impartial. In his summing-up, Judge Acton suggested that this biased jury should not be prejudiced because "some of the men had names which sounded strange". Presumably an attempt to distance the trial from any accusations of anti-Semitism.

Benny Rothman conducted his own defence

We ramblers, after a hard week's work and life in smoky towns and cities go out rambling for relaxation, a breath of fresh air, a little sunshine. We find, *when we go out, that the finest rambling country is closed to us, because certain individuals wish to shoot for about ten days a year. For twenty-five years the Ramblers' Federation has carried out a campaign which has been futile...We are not hooligans, we tried to avoid contact with the keepers by advancing in open formation. When the keepers raised their sticks we took them from them. The Mass Trespass of April 24th was a peaceful demonstration of protest.*

This was confirmed by the reporter from the *Sheffield Telegraph*, who wrote that hooliganism was completely absent. It did the ramblers little good. Anderson was found guilty of occasioning actual bodily harm and was sentenced to six months. The remainder were found guilty of riotous assembly. Benny Rothman was sent down for four months, Nussbaum for three months, and Clynes and Gillett to two months imprisonment.

The 'Establishment', in time, probably regretted the severity of these sentences, which served only to goad the rambling movement. Speaking at a rally at Winnats Pass, C.E.M Joad urged the 5000 ramblers present to become even more militant. "I should tell you that if you want the moors free, you must free them yourselves."

Mass trespasses led directly to the creation of our National Parks and the *Countryside and Rights of Way Act*, which gave a right to roam to all of these disputed moorlands.

Each year nowadays, a celebration takes place to commemorate the Kinder Scout Mass Trespass. You can take a guided walk in the steps of the Trespassers. There is a plaque in the quarry where Benny Rothman made his speech, and a new Trespass Visitors' Centre is planned.

The late Duke of Devonshire, not long before he died, apologised for the part his family had played in restricting access to Kinder Scout, and to the injustice of the trial that followed the Mass Trespass. It has since been admitted that rambling access has made no difference at all to grouse numbers on the hills.

Benny Rothman died in 2002, a hero of the Rambling movement. He fought many more battles for rambling and social justice. This book is dedicated to Benny's memory and written in admiration for all of the Kinder Scout and Abbey Brook Trespassers, particularly those who went to prison for their beliefs.

Please don't let their sacrifices be forgotten.

The Battle of Abbey Brook – the Duke of Norfolk's Road

Five months after the Kinder Scout Mass Trespass, on 18th September 1932, there was a second mass trespass along the oft-disputed right of way known as the Duke of Norfolk's Road, in the Upper Derwent Valley, not far from Sheffield.

This time, the trespass had the blessing of the Manchester Ramblers Federation and was backed by a host of other rambling and outdoor groups. Moreover, the great rambler G.H.B. Ward gave his support, though he didn't participate because of the risk of losing his public job in the Ministry of Labour.

The Abbey Brook Mass Trespass tends to be overshadowed by the Kinder Scout affair, with its harsh gaol sentences and the revenge of the Establishment against the participants. But Abbey Brook is every bit as important, and more violence was used by gamekeepers against the ramblers.

Walking out from the suburbs of Sheffield, over 200 ramblers strode over three miles out on to the moorlands to Bar Dike, a prehistoric earthwork, where the Duke of Norfolk's Road started. Despite its proven status as a right of way, ramblers were often assaulted as they walked its length, which led to G.H.B. Ward investigating the history of the road.

Much of the surrounding Yorkshire moorlands were filched by the Duke of Norfolk and Lord Fitzwilliam after an Enclosure Act of 1811 – stolen from the people who were mostly still denied the vote. Old rights of way were largely ignored by this land grab, but Ward proved that the Duke of Norfolk's Road *was* a public highway, confirmed by the Ecclesfield Tithes and Enclosure Act of 1811. The road began as a stone track, before continuing as a footpath and bridleway.

Despite being yelled at by a gamekeeper, the ramblers continued along the way, to just by the Abbey Brook. Here, a number of keepers – one account suggests forty, another around a hundred, armed with pick shafts, tore into them, viciously striking blows on the heads and shoulders of the unarmed ramblers. Concerned at the possibility of them causing serious injury, the police, who were present, yelled at the gamekeepers to aim only at the ramblers' legs.

As the keepers regrouped for another assault, most of the ramblers – feeling they had achieved their aim of walking the right of way – decided to retrace their steps.

But not all of them. A dozen, including the campaigner Howard Hill, who many years later was to write a memorable account of the day in his fine book *Freedom to Roam*, decided to press on, away from any right of way, across forbidden ground to Howshaw Tor, Bradfield Gate Head and Foulstone Depth.

The main body of the ramblers headed back the way they had come. A request to the police by the Duke of Devonshire's head gamekeeper to arrest the ramblers was ignored. The authorities were no doubt remembering the huge public backlash against the convictions of the Kinder Scout trespassers, and were probably aware that, thanks to the evidence about the road's status proven by G.H.B. Ward, that the ramblers had been subject to Common Law Assault and Battery on a public highway.

Ramblers had to wait until 1955 for the road to be put on the map as an official right of way, thanks to the legislation of the National Park and Access to the Countryside Act – one of the many gifts of Prime Minister Attlee's post-war Labour Government.

Notes for Prospective Trespassers

*What follows should **not** be taken as an incitement to trespass. I know what I do. The notes below explain some of my methods. If you want to do the same then that is your choice. As I wrote as the beginning of this book **"On your own head be it!"***

The simple fact is that most trespasses pass off without incident. In my own long career of interloping, I can think of only a small number of occasions when I've come into conflict with a landowner. Nine times out of ten you never see anyone. You may well stray on to private land either inadvertently, during the course of a country ramble, or deliberately, when you see a stretch of countryside that looks to be worth exploring. You do it, you go there, and nobody will ever know.

A lot of landowners, particularly farmers, don't mind people walking on their land. They are used to it, particularly if their land is near to a town or village. They are enlightened with the recognition that people, their neighbours, want to walk in the countryside. As long as you are well-behaved, shut the gates, and don't cause damage, disturb livestock or drop litter, they don't mind.

But then there are the other landowners. Those who hold sway over vast tracts of our countryside and don't want to share it at all. You know the kind, the ones whose land is festooned with private notices, the parklands and shooting estates. Very often, in my experience, they are newcomers to the countryside. The kind who move in and then try to keep everyone else out, often going so far as to try to close or divert public rights of way.

These are the people on whose lands you need to tread warily. In order not to be caught, you have to adopt the tactics of the old-time poachers.

Their lands are usually well worth exploring.

The first rule to being an efficient trespasser is to be a very good rambler. You need to be experienced in the art of country walking. You particularly need to be able to navigate very well with a map and compass. You need to know and understand the countryside.

If you are not at that point yet, then it is a good idea to take up rambling first. It's worth joining a rambling group. Not only will they take you out for walks in your own county, but there will usually be somebody who will teach you the rudiments of map and compass work. If you are unclubbable, you need to teach yourself, either through books or on a course.

The first trespass should always be close to home, preferably on land that isn't disputed too much. A walk around a neighbouring farm or estate will give you confidence. Early trespassers, the outlaws, the poachers, those who resisted land enclosure, didn't travel far in order to trespass. They were exploring, literally, their own 'neck of the woods'.

Keep away from houses, particularly isolated homes. People seen acting suspiciously, near to where people live are usually considered to be burglars. The good trespasser avoids alarming the innocent.

Animals will often give away the position of the trespasser, so fields with livestock are best avoided. Cattle and horses are incredibly curious. If they see a human being, they will usually run in his or her direction. Sheep mostly – but not always – run away from people.

Birds are a good indicator of the human presence. Curlews will skeer away with an alarm call. Pheasants often remain quiet until you are almost upon them, before moving off with a great cry of noise. Pigeons will divert from their flight course if they pass over a walker. Blackbirds will trill a very noisy alarm call if you disturb them.

Gamekeepers, in particular, are very skilled at using the reactions of birds and beasts to tell if someone is afoot in their game preserves. This works, of course, the other way too. The wary trespasser uses exactly the same methods to tell if a landowner or keeper is in the vicinity.

If the ground is unknown to you, then you can prepare for your trespassing walk by studying a large scale Ordnance Survey map. I favour the 1:25,000, or roughly two and a half inches to the mile scale. These OS maps show woods, footpaths and bridleways, rivers, field boundaries – all the information you need.

As I've said above, it is most important to be able to read one accurately, so that the landscape becomes a picture in your mind. Practise, practise, practise!

How to dress? Well, like a rambler, but in muted shades. There's no place here for the more garish fluorescent colours you see on some country walkers. Personally, I don't believe walkers going anywhere should stick out like sore thumbs, to the irritation of other users of the countryside.

If you are going to try camouflage, then please don't go over the top. You are a country walker, not a poacher or a member of the SAS. Do not carry any sort of weapon for similar reasons. I do favour a walking stick, which might be used to fend off ferocious dogs, and which is a useful tool to have anyway on a country walk.

You can get away with lots if you try to look like a birdwatcher. For some reason, many landowners and keepers think of twitchers as harmless eccentrics, and generally leave them alone.

Remember, many landowners don't mind casual walkers as long as they look as though they are well-behaved and not doing anything suspicious. A case can be made out for walking as though you own the place; particularly if you are respectably dressed. Gamekeepers and estate labourers may well think you are a friend of the owner.

As you walk into an area, get into the habit of continually looking all around. Take note of your route, so that you can retrace your steps if you have to. See how the land lies in all directions as you go, in case you have to work out escape routes. If you want to avoid being seen, keep in or on the edge of woodlands and stay away from the middle of fields. Use hedgerows as cover and notice quick ways out of enclosed areas. Stop and listen, every now and then, to see if anyone is about. Never walk through growing crops.

Stay off skylines as much as possible. Walkers are very visible when they are silhouetted against the sky. Keep still if you stray into an area where there are people about. If your way is definitely blocked by them, either retreat along your original route or work your way round them. Remember that the sound of footsteps can carry quite a way on frosty days when the ground is hard, or when the earth is hardened during heatwaves and droughts. Crossing streams and muddy areas can be noisy as well.

Meeting the landowner or the keeper? If it happens, you need to read their character. Are they curious or annoyed? Livid and threatening? There is no need to seek a row. You could lie that you got lost, straying off a path. Politely ask the way back to the nearest public highway. You might even make a friend. It does sometimes happen.

If they are confrontational, state politely that you will leave if they will point the way to the nearest footpath, bridleway or country lane. It's no good arguing the toss with someone carrying a shotgun or other weapon, who looks as though they might be tempted to use it. Better to live and trespass another day. If they are unarmed and unthreatening, you might want to debate the ethics of free-roaming. Personally, I think it's a waste of time.

Perhaps one day, all of this will be unnecessary and we will enjoy the same right to roam as the people north of the border, in Scotland. You can do a lot by getting involved in the wider movement and hastening that day along.

Bear in mind too, that the law of trespass may change. The present British government is seeking to make trespass a criminal rather than a civil offence – a move that must be most vigorously resisted.

Forbidden Britain

The people of Britain shouldn't need to trespass at all in order to visit their own land – the best bits of Britain. The Scottish people now have some of the best access in Europe. They may wander freely across almost all of their own land, given a few common-sense restrictions such as avoiding gardens and the immediate policies of people's homes, growing crops and so forth.

How long will it be before the peoples of England, Wales and Ireland have the same freedom?

It's true that in England and Wales we have the CRoW (*Countryside and Rights of Way Act*). This gives access on foot – with certain restrictions – to mountain and moorland, heathlands, downlands and common land. At the time, it was a step in the right direction. I campaigned for it; even though I have never really favoured this gradualist approach. Looking back over this past decade, I think it was a mistake to accept anything less than access with land reform on the Scottish model.

I welcome an annual celebration of the Kinder Scout Mass Trespass. The deeds of Benny Rothman and his fellow trespassers must never be forgotten.

But where are the mass trespasses of today?

Why are we not highlighting the forbidden woodlands? Why are we not targeting the downlands exempted from CRoW? Why are we being gradualist at all?

When I was younger, the Ramblers Association held – each year – a Forbidden Britain day. It achieved massive publicity and kept the whole subject of public access to OUR countryside on the public agenda. Sadly, some elements in the RA watered down the concept. Now it doesn't exist at all.

So shouldn't we bring it back? I say, yes!

On the weekend nearest to the Kinder Scout Mass Trespass anniversary, we should hold a Forbidden Britain Day, highlighting some appalling restriction on our right to roam. We should tell our politicians that we want nothing less than the land access enjoyed by the people of Scotland. And, if the landowning lobbies don't like it, tough! Let us slash the subsidies their members receive, care of we hard-working taxpayers. Let us make ANY subsidy conditional on free public access to the land we are paying for.

Do you remember those words of John Stuart Mill? *"No man made the land, it is the original inheritance of the whole species. The land of every country belongs to the people of that country."*

So, if you are a member of the Ramblers Association, or a political party, why not campaign within those organisations for Land Reform, with full public access to our countryside?

The need to trespass should be consigned to the history books, replaced by an absolute right to roam. And, in the meantime, let us all walk the landscapes of England, Wales and Ireland, as if we already had the land access that the Scots enjoy.

At the 2019 General Election, the winning Conservative Party – siding with the wealthy landowners who fund their political activities – stated in their manifesto an intention to criminalise trespass. While ostensibly aimed at preventing camping by Romany folk and other travellers, there is no doubt in my mind that the powers that be are intending to turn their fire on the majority of the British people, who have a long tradition of wandering freely across their own land.

Such a move must be opposed by every freedom-loving British wanderer, with direct action and mass trespasses where necessary.

I look forward to the day when the need to trespass is consigned to history, where England and Wales have Land Reform and access on the access model enjoyed in Scotland. To a day when the life and times of the Compleat Trespasser are just nostalgic memories.

ENJOY YOUR COUNTRYSIDE!

Useful Organisations

The Ramblers Association: The RA, or The Ramblers, as they prefer to be known these days, campaigns for improved access to the countryside and fights to keep open public rights of way. Their network of local groups organises walks in the British countryside. You can join online at their website www.ramblers.org.uk

The Open Spaces Society: (formally The Commons, Open Spaces and Footpaths Preservation Society) is Britain's oldest national conservation body, founded in 1865. Join online at their website www.oss.org.uk

The Land is Ours: Campaigns for fairer use of our land. www.tlio.org.uk

Recommended Reading

The traditions of trespassing in Britain are well documented. Many of these books are, sadly, out of print, but most can be obtained through your local library, or through website book dealers.

***Freedom to Roam* by Howard Hill**, Moorland Publishing, Derbyshire 1980. Despite the fact that Howard Hill's book has been overtaken by events, it is still the best historical introduction to the struggle for access to our countryside. Highly recommended.

***The 1932 Kinder Scout Trespass* by Benny Rothman**, Willow Publishing, Timperley 1982. Benny Rothman was one of the leaders of the 1932 mass trespass on to Kinder Scout, which forged the way for the eventual National Parks Act and Countryside and Rights of Way Act. This is Benny's own account of that glorious day, his subsequent trial before a loaded jury, and his spell of imprisonment - gaoled for walking across his own countryside. Don't miss reading it. *Now in a splendid new edition as well. Well worth getting as well as the original, a superb read – a goodly reminder of where we have come from on land access and where we should be going. Order a copy today!* **"The Battle for Kinder Scout" by Benny Rothman. Introduction by Mike Harding. Willow Publishing (Altrincham, Cheshire, 2012) ISBN 978-0-946361-44-1)**

***Forbidden Land* by Tom Stephenson**, Manchester University Press 1989. Good on most aspects of the history of the struggle for access to the countryside but suspect in its judgement on mass trespassing.

***Freedom to Roam* by Harold Sculthorpe**, Freedom Press, London 1993. This slim booklet takes an anarchical view of the access struggle, in a series of entertaining essays. A good follow-up to the other texts.

***A Right to Roam* by Marion Shoard**, London 1999. Now out of date, but worth looking at for the history of how the British people were denied access to their countryside.

***A Charter for Ramblers* by C.E.M Joad**, Hutchinson 1934. A key text for understanding the access battles of the twenties and thirties.

***Our Forbidden Land* by Fay Godwin.** Jonathan Cape. Superbly illustrated with Fay Godwin's black and white photographs with great text and annotations. Well worth seeking out.

***The Long Affray: The Poaching Wars in Britain* by Harry Hopkins**. The classic and definitive work on this topic. Scholarly, but very readable.

***The Poacher and the Squire* by Charles Chenevix Trench**. Longmans 1967. A good historical survey of the long-running battle between the landed and the landless, explains the way that land became forbidden thanks to the preservation of game.

***The Amateur Poacher* and *The Gamekeeper at Home* by Richard Jefferies.** Many editions. Gives a good idea of access restrictions in the game preserves of Victorian England.

***The Return of John Macnab* by Andrew Greig**, Headline London 1996. An entertaining novel that deals with some aspects of the access struggle in Scotland in the days prior to their splendid access legislation.

***The Gentle Art of Tramping* by Stephen Graham.** First published in the 1920s. Details the idea of a trespassing walk. Republished in 2019.

***Scholar Gipsies* by John Buchan**, Many editions. A delightful and inspiring book of essays and short stories on the vagabond life. John Buchan, as well as being a noted novelist, diplomat, and historian, was a devoted walker.

***Wild Country* by Sylvia Sayer**, Dartmoor Preservation Association c2001. This short text looks at why we need to preserve wild countryside and our National Parks. Well worth seeking out. Lady Sayer was a true visionary and a great advocate of freedom to roam.

***A Shepherd's Life* by W.H.Hudson,** Many editions. This beautiful account of the lives of rural folk on the Wiltshire Downs is well worth reading. It gives some account of how the people were banished from the countryside, and there is a great deal of country lore.

Guerilla Warfare* by Yank Levy, *Penguin 1941, but recent reprint. Written originally for the Home Guard, but there is a lot of useful information in this if you want to do a bit of surreptitious trespassing.

***Rambling – Some Thoughts on Country Walking* by John Bainbridge**. A celebration of the joys of the rambling life, with a chapter on trespassing days and ways.

***Wayfarer's Dole* by John Bainbridge.** A memoir of my walking days.

BY THE SAME AUTHOR

Walking Books
Wayfarer's Dole
Footloose in Devon
Footloose with George Borrow
Rambling – Some Thoughts on Country Walking

Novels
Balmoral Kill
Dangerous Game
Loxley
Wolfshead
Villain
Legend
The Shadow of William Quest
Deadly Quest
Dark Shadow

John's walking blog www.walkingtheoldways.wordpress.com

John's writing blog www.johnbainbridgewriter.wordpress.com

Printed in Great Britain
by Amazon